in 1~~......................~~ he has worked for numerous wineries and is now director of Liquid Ideas, a national wine consultancy business based in Melbourne. Stuart writes for *australian good taste* magazine, the *Sunday Telegraph* and the *Sunday Herald Sun*, and has a regular spot on ABC Radio 774.

Xmas
2003
est
Christophe,
The Bonne
Viveur,
Here's to
fine glugging
in 2004!
Much love as
always from Liz
xxxxx

Enjoy the book

Cheers

Stuart Gregor

★ ★ ★ ★ ★

don't buy wine without me

australia's best value drinking 2004

stuart gregor

t

text publishing melbourne australia

The Text Publishing Company
171 La Trobe Street
Melbourne Victoria 3000
Australia

First published 2003

Printed and bound by BPA Print Group
Designed by Chong
Typeset in 10/12 Adobe Garamond by J & M Typesetting

National Library of Australia
Cataloguing-in-Publication data:

Gregor, Stuart.
 Don't buy wine without me: Stuart Gregor's wine guide 2004.

 ISBN 1 877008 82 6

 1. Wine and wine making – Australia – Guidebooks. I. Title. II. Title: Wine
guide 2003.

641.872

contents

Acknowledgments

It is important to note that all of the wines that appear in the book are tasted blind by me and invariably a group of well-educated wine palates. I would like to thank the following people who tasted wines with me this year.

Angie Bradbury, Cameron Mackenzie, Kate Goodman, Llawela Forrest, Sarah Scorpo, Phil Kerney, Greg Dedman, Kathleen Quealy, Matthew Parish, Steve Flamsteed, Grant van Every, Melissa Moore, Nick Morris, Alex Wilcox, Erez Gordon, Alison Shier.

Several of the wines recommended in this book are produced by clients of Liquid Ideas. As with all the others, they were tasted 'blind', invariably in the company of other judges, and were included on merit.

I dedicate this book to the grape growers of Australia who do all the hard work.

Symbols

★ ★ ★ to ★ ★ ★ ☆ Great quality and value wine. Better than probably 90% of the wines on the market.

★ ★ ★ ★ to ★ ★ ★ ★ ☆ Getting into special territory here. Fabulous wine that really delivers all you could possibly want in terms of both quality and value.

★ ★ ★ ★ ★ Rush down to your local bottle shop and buy as much of these wines as you can cram in the boot.

🗲 The wine is available with a screwcap (but may also be available with a cork).

🍷 Sweeter than you might be expecting.

ⓕ (red) Full flavoured red—probably has plenty of fruit and a bit of oak. Drink with steaks, stews, raw game and your butchest friends.

Ⓜ (red) Medium weight. More civilised than the monsters, often a bit more fun and you won't need to wear a seatbelt.

Ⓛ (red) Light but not necessarily insubstantial—some of the lighter reds are the most complex and intellectual. Drink with an art critic.

ⓕ (white) A big, fat, comforting white you could have with roast chicken. Or veal casserole; or pizza, or…just about anything really.

Ⓜ (white) Not too heavy, not too light; multi-purpose and just about right.

Ⓛ (white) Zingy, springy, tangy and tantalising. Easy on the brain and the palate. Drink with a song in your heart.

Welcome to *Don't Buy Wine Without Me* 2004

This year's edition is bigger, brighter and better than ever with more reviews, more information and more tips to make your wine buying even easier.

This year we have spread our price points a little further to make sure you buy the best wines for yourselves at the best prices, but that you also know exactly what to buy when you scale the lofty peaks of Over-$20 Land.

We have updated the Winespeak section so you can decipher some of those back labels, tasting notes and wine columns. We have improved the Regions section too; so if you are travelling to any of Australia's wine regions—don't go without me!

And of course as ever we have cut straight to the point.

There is not a bad wine in this book—less than 20% of the wines I have tasted this year appear in these pages. So if you feel inclined to ask yourself—gee, I wonder why such and such isn't in the book, the answer is simple. It wasn't good enough.

As usual the value of the wine is of the utmost importance—sure, it might be good but is it overpriced? If so (and excepting the odd iconic wine that just can't be ignored) you won't see it in these pages.

Great wine at a ridiculously good price? Just look for the four- and five- star wines and seek them out on the shelves.

So what do you need to know to navigate the book this year?

★ Well, firstly you should check out the guide to symbols on page 1. The ⑤ is new—it means that the wine, or at least a percentage of the wine, has been bottled under screwcap. My advice *on all occasions* is try to find the screwcap version. Screwcaps are the future and you shouldn't be afraid to embrace them or—worse—be snobby about them. On the contrary, grip them tight, unscrew them and revel in the fact that the wine will always taste exactly how its maker intended. Because despite pulling-up-of-socks noises from the cork producers, we still open far too many wines spoiled by cork taint. (Skip ahead to *corked wines* in the Winespeak section for more on this.)

★ Again this year we have given you an indication of the weight of a wine and—for those wines that sit in the main sections alongside mostly dry wines—a clue that it is a little bit on the sweet side.

★ This year we have again featured the Gregor star system. Page 1 gives a guide to interpreting the stars (and yes, your aspect probably is in Uranus this week), but it is also important to remember that the star system works on the basis of quality *plus* value. So you might be surprised to see a $6 wine receive five stars, but it's because I reckon for that price, the wine is AWESOME value. Maybe not as high quality in absolute terms as a $20 wine with four stars—but there again, once you've drunk three bottles of the cheap one you'll never know the difference!

★ 2003 has certainly been the year of the screwcap. I know I said something very similar about 2002, but this was the year that the screwcap stopped being something unusual perched atop the odd bottle of riesling and became more common on other white varieties and even some reds. There are many more wines sealed by screwcap in the book this year, and I'm pretty sure that in a couple of years I'll have as many screwcapped wines in these pages as there are under cork. We can only hope—and exercise our purchasing power.

★ 2003 was also the year that the summer bushfires had a real effect on the wine harvest. The drought already meant that most grape growers were going to harvest lower yields than normal but the fires, particularly in the north-east of Victoria, made things even worse. Not only were yields down but when the grapes started fermenting they gave off this rather obvious smoke aroma. It seems the smoke had infiltrated the grape skins, and things looked like going from bad to worse. But the wine industry is two things—ingenious and loyal. So some wine technical companies quickly worked out some clever ways to reduce the smoky flavours and most winemakers still paid for the grapes even if they were never going to be good enough to make any final blends.

★ Among other trends to keep an eye out for is (I can't believe I am writing this) the improvement in the quality of most merlot in Australia. But there is a caveat to this comment and it's a bit of an odd one. Stick to cheap merlot and you'll be okay—I reckon the best ones tend to be under $20. When winemakers stuff around trying to make Grange out of merlot it normally results in disaster but when they set out happily to make fresh, fruity, simple red wine it seems to work out much better.

Best Value Drinking Awards 2004

This year we've decided to give credit where it's due (because if there's anything we know about here at *Don't Buy Wine Without Me*, it's credit) and have instigated a list of awards to recognise the producers of the best-value wines in the country. Each of these award-winning wines provides almost criminal value for money and should be a staple in every drinker's cellar or fridge over the next twelve months. And so, without further ado…

winery of the year 2004

De Bortoli Wines, Yarra Valley and Griffith

De Bortoli is our 2004 Winery of the Year for this simple reason: through their entire range, from their cheapest wine through to the posh stuff, value for money is always paramount. This great family-owned winery has two homes—one in the workhorse Riverina region and the other in the rather more glamorous Yarra Valley, and the wines from both homes are consistently excellent. Whether it is the $6 Montage range or a Yarra Valley chardonnay of genuine class, you can't go past a De Bortoli wine for a sure thing.

best value sparkling wine 2004

Yellowglen Vintage Pinot Noir Chardonnay 2001 $13–15

The sparkling wines of Yellowglen have never been better and this is an Aussie bubble that should keep the party set extremely well lubricated throughout summer. The sparkling wine category has been the domain of the winemakers from Hardys over recent years so it is great to see someone giving them a bit of competition. Yellowglen is traditionally a soft and elegant sparkler rather than a big, rich style, so it is perfect for all manner of celebrations.

best value white wine 2004

West End Richland Sauvignon Blanc 2003 $9–11

This gets white wine of the year on two counts, the first being that it is clearly a terrific example of sauvignon blanc at a drop-dead giveaway price. The second is that it's the second in a row from this little Griffith winery. The 2002 was such a knockout I never expected them to be able to follow it up with an equally good version in 2003—I should never have doubted. Pick this up by the armful and devour it with your favourite seafood.

best value red wine 2004

Yalumba Merlot 2002 $9–11

Less than twelve months after dismissing all merlot as undrinkable swill I am now elevating one to the podium as my best-value red wine of the year. Some people might suggest this is a true reflection of my fragile mindset but I like to see it as giving credit where it's due (see above) and also making a cogent point about merlot—the best ones are the cheap ones. This is a delicious red wine that combines richness and character with an almost unbeatable price. Should be a compulsory house wine.

best value sweet wine 2004

Seppelt Tokay DP 37 $18–20

Can you imagine any other category of food or drink in the world where you would get the following deal? Brand X, that already makes a wonderful product at a very good price, decides to undergo a repackaging exercise in which it *doubles* the size of the product and *doesn't increase the price*. It's madness. Last year this wine was 375 mL of world-class tokay (except that no one else in the world makes tokay like this) for around $20, this year it is 750 mL of peerless tokay for around $20. So no other sweet wine comes near this for value—except maybe the muscat under the same label, which has had exactly the same treatment.

top quality
& great value

casks

The quality of cask wine in Australia has never been better but there are a couple of important things to note. Wine doesn't keep as well in a bag as it does in a bottle. Check the best-before date and buy the wine with the date furthest away—it will be freshest.

The quality of white wine casks is far superior to the vast majority of reds and the same goes for the two-litre versus four-litre debate—it's just a fact that the smaller casks are better in almost all circumstances.

Banrock Station Cabernet Merlot

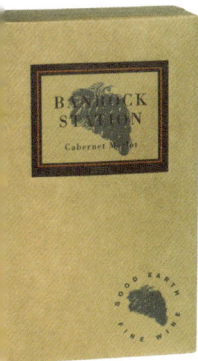

People keep telling me there is a glut of red wine in the marketplace, meaning prices are being pushed down to their lowest level in a decade. This surely would mean that the quality of cask wines should increase as the better fruit gets cheaper. Is there any evidence of this happening? Well, not just yet but I suspect as we progress through 2004 we might notice a step up in quality. Mind you this little plummy number isn't bad at all right now—if it gets any better I'll be drinking it instead of the cheap bottles.

$13–15 2L

Banrock Station Chardonnay

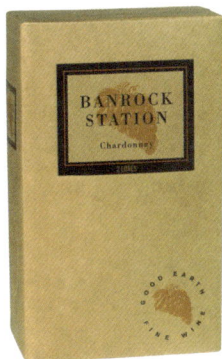

Buying Banrock Station wines helps save all the birdies and the river-loving things on the banks of the Murray River, courtesy of the winery's well-publicised wetlands project. In all seriousness, the Murray–Darling system has been struggling for some time, and projects like this help keep it alive and thriving. This is nice varietal, peachy chardonnay—a perfectly acceptable fridge-door filler and a small contribution to the health of the environment.

$13–15 2L

Hardy's Regional Reserve Shiraz

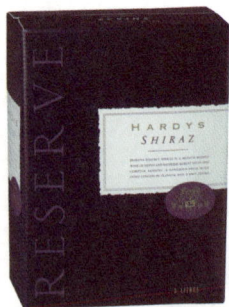

The Hardy's Regional Reserve collection has been a successful, good-value bottled wine for many years and the tradition has been carried on in the bag-in-a-box. This is no blockbuster shiraz but it is a fresh and fruity, medium-bodied red that wouldn't be a bad introduction for people who are just starting out in the world of red wine. Also if I was making a big stew (which in fact I hardly ever do) I would happily use plenty of this wine in the cooking and equally happily drink the rest.

$12–14 2L

Yalumba Colombard Chardonnay

When I worked on the bottle shop floor a decade ago this was our biggest selling two-litre cask by a mile. Everyone used to love it (including the impoverished staff) because it was always fresh and crisp, and not too sweet like some of the other white casks. A decade on, this wine is still leading the pack and all credit to the canny cask drinkers for sussing out the best one and sticking with it. And a bit of credit to Yalumba for keeping up the standards.

$10–12 2L

Yalumba Sauvignon Blanc

I reckon the wine we tasted for this book might have been the last of the 2002 vintage. The next vintage swings in at the end of 2003 and if it's even half as good as the 2002 it will be better than most of the casks on the market. The 2002 had great, lifted, zesty sauvignon blanc characters and certainly tasted like the real thing. By the way, if you do find a 2002 vintage tucked away somewhere, remember to make sure the best-before date is at least six months away.

$11–13 2L

sparklings

Okáy I have a confession to make—apart from my professional responsibilities, like tastings for this book, I don't drink an awful lot of sparkling wine. Oh sure, weddings are an exception, but after a glass or two I'm the bloke craning his neck to find a beer or a glass of red. Nonetheless, like most drinkers (and all drunks) I know what I like. When I look for good sparkling wines I like fresh, clean flavours, not the slightest hint of bitterness and nothing too sweet. A little bit of sugar admittedly makes the medicine go down and it certainly doesn't hurt in a nice glass of bubbles; but the sweetness must be in balance with the acidity so the wine still tastes fresh and not sickly sweet.

Andrew Garrett Pinot Noir Chardonnay NV

★ ★ ★ ★ ★

Andrew Garrett, the man, hasn't had anything to do with this wine for more than a decade so maybe this should be called the Chilly Hargrave, because he's the guy who actually makes it, not Andrew. If that doesn't make sense, make sense of this: this is a crackerjack sparkling wine, made in just the elegant style that I like. It is well balanced, not too sweet and just perfect for an afternoon party in spring with lots of Dandy Andys and not too Chilly Willys.

$12–14

Banrock Station Reserve Sparkling Shiraz NV

★ ★ ★ ★ ★

If you drink Banrock Station you will go to heaven because a percentage of all sales goes to saving the wetlands on the banks of the Murray. You see I have finally been brainwashed by the marketing department at Hardys. I am a drone. And I even like the wine, in fact this is now close to the best inexpensive sparkling red in the country. Rich and full of plum and cherry flavours, a perfect primer for those who are dubious about the charms of bubbly red.

$13–15

{sparklings} 13

Blue Pyrenees Midnight Cuvée 1999

★ ★ ★ ★ ☆

Perhaps a fraction on the dear side for our standard bubbles section? Since I have drunk more of this sparkling wine than almost any other Australian bubbles in the past twelve months, I can't really think of it as a wine to save for *very* special occasions. Made from 100% chardonnay, it has a noticeably soft and sweet palate that just makes it quaffable beyond belief. Be careful with this wine—I have friends who are addicted.

$26–30

Brown Brothers Pinot Noir & Chardonnay NV

★ ★ ★ ★ ☆

The Browns are better known for just about everything other than sparklings but this is an absolute belter of a bubble. Browns own some of the coolest and highest vineyards in the country, meaning they can get exceptionally fine grapes for sparkling wine base every year. All the fruit for this wine comes from the King Valley and surrounds, and deft winemaking has made it complex, really lovely on the palate and beautifully balanced.

$16–18

Jansz NV
★ ★ ★ ★

Most of the best bubbles in Australia come from Tassie, including the Jansz NV. There is also an excellent vintage Jansz and a late-disgorged Jansz which creep over $25, but this is the best value in the range to my mind. The beauty of the non-vintage wine is that you are not dependent entirely on the vagaries of one season, you can blend across the years to make sure consistency of style is retained. This wine is fresh and apple-y with just a hint of yeasty complexity.

$18–22

Omni NV
★ ★ ★ ★

When they launched the mighty Omni in a litre bottle last year at Christmas, I thought all my Christmases had come at once. It was a great idea because this wine gets a run when there are plenty of people around and the bigger the bottle the better. The fact that the winemakers at Hardys can sell a litre of such a good bubble for about ten bucks is a tribute to their genius. And if you like your bubble a bit sweeter, look out for the new Omni Blue.

$10–12 (1 litre bottle available at Christmas)

Seaview Pinot Noir Chardonnay Vintage Reserve Brut 1998

★ ★ ★ ★ ★

This is a wine that has pretensions to greater things, a wine, quite frankly, that thinks it should be a damn sight more expensive than it is. And it's right. This wine shows real champagne characters of yeast and toast and has some bottle development as well. The result is a genuinely rich and complex bubbles that I reckon you could decant into a Bollinger bottle and no one would notice the difference.

$18–20

Seppelt Sparkling Shiraz 1999

★ ★ ★ ★

Year in, year out, this remains almost too good to be true. Full but complex and slightly spicy, with an attractive hint of dryness following the fizzy red fruit, this is said to be the perfect partner for the Christmas turkey. But it's also good to have simply as a celebration at the end of a meal. Most of us don't drink stickies or port with dessert any more, so why not pop a bottle of the red bubbles—it's sweet enough and rather more exciting. Go on, be a devil—a little red one.

$16–18

Sir James Pinot Noir Chardonnay NV

★ ★ ★ ★

The Sir James bubbles maintain their standards like a British officer maintains his stiff upper lip. Sir James Hardy was a great sailor and a terrific wine man and the sparklers that bear his name are testament to the commitment of Ed Carr and the wonderful team at Hardys to lead the market. It's a tall order, and I do get the feeling that the rest of the field is at last starting to catch up. But this is still an unbeatable aperitif before you head out on the yacht.

$12–14

Sir James Pinot Noir Chardonnay Vintage 1999

★ ★ ★ ★ ☆

Another in the classic mould from Hardys, and when this wine is on special in the teens, it's one of the best buys in the country. Hardys makes more expensive bubbles than this, including the $50-plus Arras, but this is the wine that most often impresses. So don't go out and buy Arras, buy three bottles of this instead—you won't taste the difference, you'll feel smarter and you'll be drinking with a few more friends.

$20–23

[sparklings] 17

Yellow

★ ★ ★ ★ ☆

When Yellow by Yellowglen came onto the market a few years back it created a storm with its groovy, striking label. What I like, however, is that the wine inside is not a gimmick. It's a bit sweeter than the Yellowglen pinot chardonnay, but still a fresh and fruity style, aimed fairly and squarely at pleasing all palates. The Yellow has recently been joined by a Red and a Pink and they're both okay, too.

$11–13

Yellowglen Vintage Pinot Noir Chardonnay 2001

[best value sparkling] ★ ★ ★ ★ ★

Yellowglen has been a staple of the bubble-loving set for an eternity; in fact if you go back twenty years it was the first serious challenger to Minchinbury and Barossa Pearl. Last year for the first time Yellowglen became a vintage wine, meaning all the fruit comes from the same year, which seems only to have improved the product. This pinot noir chardonnay is delicate, fresh and quite dry—a lovely style that will keep everyone smiling.

$13–15

whites

There is more good-value white wine in Australia than ever at the moment so let me simply counsel you to buy up big over summer. Riesling continues to be a star buy and should remain so, since I'm told the great riesling boom is now over; but the chardonnays available at competitive prices are improving at a cracking pace. And I still believe, even though no one listens, that at $15 or so the best wines by far are made from semillon. Try a semillon, just for a change. Go on, it won't kill you (if it does *Don't Buy Wine Without Me* takes no responsibility).

Alkoomi Riesling 2002

★ ★ ★ ★

Alkoomi was the founding father of the Frankland River region of Western Australia; now the Frankland is fast becoming one of the hottest regions in the country with producers big and small eyeing off its near-perfect climate and wide open expanses of land. The Alkoomi wines are characterised by their wonderful searing acidity, which makes them fresh as a daisy and lively on the palate. This riesling is no exception—fine, delicate and beautifully crisp.

$17–19 Ⓛ 🥄

Andrew Garrett Chardonnay 2002

★ ★ ★ ★ ☆

Andrew Garrett wines have improved recently under the guidance of the winemakers at Beringer Blass. This one used to be big, round and simple (sort of me in a bottle) but now it is quite refined with lovely barrel aromas and flavours, and some complexity on the palate. The sort of chardonnay that might make you ask yourself why you haven't been drinking more chardonnay lately. If it's because people like me keep telling you to drink riesling, ignore me—I'm an idiot.

$13–15 Ⓜ

Angove's Bear Crossing Chardonnay 2002

★ ★ ★ ★

Sometimes I get a bit guilty in wine shops. There I am enjoying myself; but what if they had to cut a tree down to plant this vineyard and the tree had a koala in it and it fell out and landed on its head…So to ease my mind I buy this fresh and peachy chardonnay knowing that a little of my coin goes to rescuing the koalas that fall out of trees. And the best thing is that it's a really lovely, fruity chardonnay that is almost impossible not to quaff. Just beware of the drop bears.

$8–10 Ⓜ

Annabella Moscato 2002

★ ★ ★ ☆

Unfazed by the collapse of their 'Wicked' wines which, although quite nice, were hardly wicked in the skateboarding sense, the good folk at BRL Hardy have morphed Wicked into Annabella. I hate to think of the market research that went into choosing the name, but the wine is a classic moscato style and as such is delicious and very sensible. Low in alcohol, slightly sweet and with a little fizz on the tongue, this is the ideal morning or late-afternoon-get-in-the-mood wine.

$12–13 Ⓛ 🦋

Annie's Lane Semillon 2002
★ ★ ★ ★

The Clare Valley has a largely unheralded ability to make really good semillon and Annie's Lane makes one of the best. Some of the vineyards that produce this wine are fifty years old and were responsible for many of the great Quelltaler hock wines of the 1960s. If you missed the 60s, rest assured that you can still catch this wine in all its delightful freshness, particularly if you come across one of the screwcapped bottles. Hints of lemon and straw, and absolutely more-ish.

$14–16 Ⓜ 🥄

Ashwood Grove Sauvignon Blanc 2002
★ ★ ★ ☆

This wine is one example among many of the quality of 2002 sauvignon blanc from the warm regions. They might be starting to run out by now though, so I suggest you buy up some cheap '02 sauvignon blanc before the end of the year if you can. And since it doesn't cellar all that well, I recommend drinking it before the start of the 2004 vintage in February. That may not sound like a giant-sized window of opportunity, but a positive attitude will get you a long way.

$12–13 Ⓛ

Best's Great Western Riesling 2002

★ ★ ★ ★ ☆

The Best's rieslings from 2002 are the best I've ever tasted from this winery (sorry) and this one goes to prove you can make terrific riesling in some of the most unlikely places. It also helps to support my pet theory that where you can grow great shiraz you should also be able to grow great riesling—they like the same conditions and soils. This is fine and flinty with some lovely floral notes, and should force you to reassess your riesling regional prejudices.

$18–20 Ⓛ ⑤

Best's Victoria Riesling 2002

★ ★ ★ ★ ★

Hidden away up in Great Western, Victoria, the Thompson family of Best's have been crafting lovely wines for decades without ever making headlines. This wine, however, must be brought to people's attention—it is a terrific riesling with floral and honeysuckle notes, as good as anything under $20. If you want to support a lovely family doing what they do extremely well and without much fuss, seek this one out.

$11–13 Ⓛ ⑤

Brokenwood Cricket Pitch Sauvignon Blanc Semillon 2002

★ ★ ★ ★

The Cricket Pitch has been a staple for many years now and it is good to see they have never dropped the ball (get it? Cricket pitch—ball…) At the start of 2003 Brokenwood boss Iain Riggs decided his Cricket Pitch white and red, as well as most of his chardonnay and pinot noir, would be bottled under screwcap. So you might find some of this wine on the shelves under cork and some of it under screwcap—buy the screwcap one and give it a little spin!

$15–17 Ⓜ

Brookland Valley Verse 1 Semillon Sauvignon Blanc 2002

★ ★ ★ ★

The Brookland Valley wines continue to impress although the bad news is that they seem to have jumped in price a bit from what I remember last year. The herbaceous sauvignon blanc and the lovely lemony semillon combine to make this a terrific wine regardless of the price. Brookland Valley is part of the greater BRL Hardy clan and the wines seem to have benefited from the association; they've only got better in the past few years. A lovely fresh summertime drink.

$17–19 Ⓜ

Cape Mentelle Semillon Sauvignon Blanc 2003

★ ★ ★ ★

Cape Mentelle is still one of the great wineries of Western Australia, such an icon that we are even prepared to forget that it is owned by the French. Cape Mentelle is one finger of the Australian arm of the Louis Vuitton Moët Hennessy group, better known as LVMH, probably the world's leading luxury goods manufacturer. Cape Mentelle is in a family that includes Krug, Moët and Chandon and Chateau d'Yquem—and the Cape Mentelle SSB is always a benchmark of style. No wonder.

$23–25 Ⓜ

Capel Vale Sauvignon Blanc Semillon 2002

★ ★ ★ ★

Capel Vale was just about my most improved winery of 2002–03 and it's nice to see that they are showing no signs of letting up on the terrific pace they set last year. This is another beautifully made, delicious wine, a wine that sets me dreaming about the South Coast, sitting on a balcony barbecueing the fresh snapper I caught that morning. Of course it was the biggest fish we caught all day…and perfect with this semillon sauvignon blanc blend.

$17–19 Ⓜ

Charles Sturt University Chardonnay 2002

★ ★ ★ ☆

The future of Australian winemaking is in pretty safe hands if the kids from the winemaking college at Charles Sturt University in Wagga can do this. The college has a fully functioning commercial winery which must give the students an enormous amount of confidence when they leave with their degrees. This chardonnay is sourced from some of the local cool vineyards around Orange and is fruit driven and well balanced with lovely acidity.

$13–14 Ⓜ ⌇

Coldstream Hills Chardonnay 2002

★ ★ ★ ★ ☆

The quality of the wines never faltered after Southcorp bought Coldstream Hills from guru wine writer James Halliday in 1996. The 2002 chardonnay is wonderfully elegant, lightly oaked and with a lovely touch of grapefruit character that marks down good cool climate fruit and clever winemaking (if you like grapefruit of course). This wine oscillates quite dramatically in price, depending on what deals Southcorp have in the system, so wait for a special and go for it.

$22–24 Ⓜ

De Bortoli Gulf Station Chardonnay 2002
★ ★ ★ ★ ★

It's possible that De Bortoli makes the best value chardonnays in the country; certainly they make the best value chardonnay in the Yarra Valley. This Gulf Station chardonnay has the cool climate finesse and structure of a wine twice its price, in fact it's better than many Yarra Valley chardonnays that *are* twice its price. If I had this wine, a piece of beautifully poached salmon and Cameron Diaz in that white bikini from *Charlie's Angels*, you wouldn't find a happier man on earth.

$17–19

De Bortoli Montage Chardonnay Semillon 2002
★ ★ ★ ☆

This is a pretty simple peachy little number, but it is also a technically excellent wine with some nice lemony character from the semillon and none of those horrible sour flavours you so often encounter in wines at this price. This is a montage of two terrific varieties done damn well, so while it may not look too pretty and the price is definitely below what you reckon constitutes a 'serious' wine, let not prejudice stand in your way. This is tops.

$7–9 Ⓛ

De Bortoli Montage Semillon Sauvignon Blanc 2002

★ ★ ★ ★ ★

You should be able to pick this wine up for $7—in one of the big stores you might go closer to $5. And that makes me proud to be Australian. This ain't no pretty bottle, this ain't no pretty label but this sure is pretty wine. A fresh, fruity, mouthful of summer fun, and if you can't find this vintage keep an eye out for the 2003. De Bortoli continues to astound with its ability to make great wine at ridiculous prices—long may they continue in the same vein.

$7–9 Ⓛ

De Bortoli Windy Peak Chardonnay 2002

★ ★ ★ ★ ☆

If the Gulf Station chardonnay from De Bortoli is Cameron Diaz then this wine is certainly Drew Barrymore. It's not quite as polished, refined or sexy as its more expensive rival but it still kicks butt in the fun stakes. Who wouldn't love a bit of Drew in a bottle? It's cheeky, pretty bloody rich and sure, it's a little bit rounder than some of its counterparts but it really makes you smile. Lovely chardonnay at a great price, in case you were wondering.

$13–15 Ⓜ

De Bortoli Yarra Valley Chardonnay 2001

★ ★ ★ ★ ☆

The 2001 vintage of this wine is running low but De Bortoli have an equally good 2002 in the wings and in any case this is a wine we couldn't leave out. When I first tasted it I thought it was a classy package; when I found out it had won trophies I was not at all surprised. When someone told me it was just a spot over $20, however, I was gobsmacked. Beautiful fruit, gorgeously high quality oak—the works!

$22–24 Ⓕ

Evans & Tate Classic 2003

★ ★ ★ ★

One of the standard bearers for this style of blended white wine, and it's good to see it has returned to top form and is being bottled very sensibly under a screwcap. The wine has a few aromas of green pea and capsicum which I like but my wife, who is capsicum intolerant, can't tolerate—it's a funny one capsicum; you either love it or hate it. On the palate this is absolutely true to type: zingy and fresh and quite uncomplicated— Margaret River's answer to Larry Emdur.

$15–17 Ⓛ ⤴

Gapsted Chardonnay 2001
★ ★ ★ ★

This is a lovely restrained, tight and very cool-climate chardonnay. Gapsted has sourced fruit for this wine from the King Valley in Victoria (pretty cool) Tumbarumba in NSW (very cool, in the Snowies) and the Alpine Valleys of Victoria (the name says it all). The result is very fine fruit flavours that have mercifully not been overwhelmed by oak. The future of high-quality chardonnay in Australia is set in cool regions but hey—why stick to just one?

$20–22 Ⓜ

Gapsted Tutu Chardonnay Verdelho 2002
★ ★ ★ ★

What the hell is a tutu doing on a wine label? According to the folk at Gapsted it is a tribute to the ballerina canopy that ensures plenty of sun gets onto the grapes in their cool King Valley vineyards. So what does a wine made from a tutu taste like? In fact, rather delicious albeit a little bit fruitier than your average ballet. More like a drag show if the truth be known, featuring a rampant Carmen Miranda with a hat full of pineapples and bananas.

$10–12 Ⓜ

Gapsted Tutu Muscato 2002

★ ★ ★ ☆

Here's a wine that will split any jury in half. It's sweet, quite low in alcohol, has a tutu on the label and it's called muscato. Based on the Italian Moscato d'Asti style, this is the ideal spring brunch drink when you're craving something slightly sweet to get the taste buds going; in fact this is a perfect wine if you are having a kids' party and lots of cup cakes. The wine's for the grown-ups, by the way.

$10–12 Ⓛ 🦋

Grant Burge Barossa Vines Semillon 2002

★ ★ ★ ★ ☆

Every year my doctor tells me I'm crazy to spout the virtues of Barossa semillon. It's too hot there to grow semillon, he tells me. Well maybe for some styles, I answer, but there should be room in the canon for this great old-fashioned style of wine. He just looks at me and writes me another prescription—it never fails. But really, this is great stuff. Lemons and toast and perfectly delicious—another victory for a downtrodden style. 'Can you hear the people sing…'

$12–14 Ⓜ

Grant Burge Summers Chardonnay 2002

★ ★ ★ ★

This wine popped up in a recent blind tasting and I loved it, marking it my top chardonnay in the tasting. The winemaker next to me didn't like it at all and gave it almost her lowest score. Why did I love this wine? Well I saw some great length on the palate and some lovely fruit and lemony acidity. She hated it because (okay I admit it) it did smell a bit funny on the nose. However it's my book and I reckon: just get past the stink bomb and this wine rocks.

$18–20 Ⓜ

Hanging Rock Verdelho 2002

★ ★ ★ ★

Verdelho is a funny thing—it just can't seem to find a home in Australia. One minute I think it's best suited to warm regions like the Hunter in NSW or the Swan Valley in WA, and then I taste it from cooler regions and I'm all confused. I'm guessing the fruit for this wine came from both warm and cool climates, and maybe that's the best option. Combine the rich, sweet fruit from the warm regions with the more tarty fresh fruit from the cool regions. The result? Delicious.

$18–20 Ⓜ

Houghton Crofters Semillon Sauvignon Blanc 2002

★ ★ ★ ★

It's easy to tell who is having a bit of trouble moving their stock by noting when wines are released. This came out around June 2003, almost a year later than some others. Which says to me that the old Crofters probably isn't the hottest item on the shelves these days. But as I have said before, don't let fashion dictate what you drink—this is a lovely wine with plenty of fruity, citrussy characters and good balance.

$18–20 Ⓜ

Houghton White Burgundy 2002

★ ★ ★ ★ ★

If the wine industry was a sport we would surely have a Hall of Fame. And after posh things like Grange were inducted I'd be putting my nomination in to give Houghton White Burgundy a place. The label will eventually have to lose the 'B' word, but don't let that worry you, this wine won't ever change.

No one seems to know what's in it, although it probably features chenin blanc, but I don't care and nor should you—just drink it. The 2002 is just as good as any vintage ever made.

$11–13 Ⓜ

Hungerford Hill Chardonnay 2002

★ ★ ★ ★

I must admit to having lost track of what's going on at Hungerford Hill. I know that Southcorp sold it and that the new winemaker is one of the people who also got short shrift in the Southcorp shenanigans. The main thing is that the price of this wine seems to have come down while the quality is as good as ever. The new owners are Cassegrain and winemaker Phillip John is doing a top job for them. Fresh, vibrant, peachy chardonnay.

$16–18 Ⓕ

Isabel Sauvignon Blanc 2003 NZ

★ ★ ★ ★

Yet another great sauvignon blanc from Marlborough. This wine comes in at the ripe end of the spectrum and thus it has full tropical fruit aromas and flavours as well as the more traditional grassy Marlborough 'cat's pee' that we have come to love. If you have a friend named Isabel she's probably a good cook who does things properly—nice napkins and matching cutlery—so you'd better buy her a bottle the next time you're over at her place for dinner.

$22–24 Ⓜ

Jacob's Creek Chardonnay 2002

★ ★ ★

Every winemaker in the country should genuflect before a picture of Jacob's Creek at least once every week. Without Jacob's Creek the Australian wine industry wouldn't be the worldwide success it is today, and it was the chardonnay that led the way— I remember drinking it in England fifteen years ago and thinking how much I missed home and all its sunny, honest flavours and its fruity, fresh chardonnay. I love Jacob's Creek.

$9–11 Ⓜ

Jamiesons Run Chardonnay 2002

★ ★ ★ ☆

Jamiesons Run is now almost as wide as the Long Paddock and as free flowing as Jacob's Creek. These wines might once have had geographical significance but not anymore, they've grown up far and wide. Even so, this chardonnay is still sourced from the Limestone Coast, probably Padthaway, and it shows that typical character of fleshy generous fruit and some nice deft, not-too-heavy handling with the oak barrels. Clever wine.

$13–15 Ⓕ

Jim Barry Watervale Riesling 2002

★ ★ ★ ★

Jim Barry and his sons Peter and Mark are characters who live large and party hard. But they also make some of the most pristine and beautiful wines in the Clare Valley and their respect for the valley's great vineyards is awe-inspiring. Every region in the country should have a few people like the Barrys to make sure the things that make the place special are preserved. This, by the way, is yet another terrific 2002 Clare riesling.

$13–15 Ⓛ ⤳

Knappstein Riesling 2002

★ ★ ★ ★

We all know that most of the Clare rieslings from the fabulous 2002 vintage have sold out by now, but here is one you should still be able to find, because for some reason it was released six months after the rest. Knappstein riesling has heaps of flavour but it is not made in the delicate style of some of the others from Clare. Perhaps it reflects the winemaker, who is known affectionately in the Valley as Ox. A wonderfully balanced wine that will age gracefully. Keep it for five years if you can.

$18–20 Ⓜ ⤳

Knight Granite Hills Riesling 2002

★ ★ ★ ★ ☆

This incredibly intense riesling is one of the best-kept secrets in Australian winemaking. The winery is located up in the Macedon Ranges, a very chilly region only half an hour's drive from Melbourne airport. The winemaker Llew Knight is an unassuming bloke whose wines do all the talking, and do it eloquently. This fine, intense, focussed riesling is one for now or for up to a decade in the cellar. A wine that will surprise and delight you—and what more could you ask?

$18–20 Ⓛ

Leasingham Bastion Riesling 2002

★ ★ ★ ★ ★

Basics of Wine Marketing 101: release a new brand with a familiar association (e.g. Leasingham), make the first vintage so sensational people will fall over themselves to buy it (e.g. the phenomenal '99 Bastion Red), and then 'line extend' by adding some whites to the range. *Voilà*! The Bastion riesling is born. This wonderful, citrussy Clare riesling shows once more how good the vintage was—and how much great fruit these big wineries can get hold of.

$9–11 Ⓛ ⑤

Leconfield Old Vine Riesling 2002

★ ★ ★ ★ ☆

Even though this wine will almost certainly be sold out by Christmas and thus may be difficult to find as you read this, I wanted to assure anyone smart and good looking enough to have bought a few bottles that it is an absolute beauty, and one of the five best rieslings from 2002. And that's not just my opinion, this wine collected trophies at a few wine shows including Adelaide, where it beat many stunning Clare wines from the same year.

$17–19 Ⓛ 〰

Lindemans Reserve Verdelho 2002

★ ★ ★ ★ ☆

Once upon a time we all held out great hopes for verdelho. It was going to be the next big thing, the new chardonnay. Then riesling became the new chardonnay—and now chardonnay is back. Where does that leave verdelho? On the shelves mostly.
But if you want a tropical-fruit flavoured wine with a real full-bodied kick then this is the wine for you. It might not be the new chardonnay, but good verdelho is still a pretty decent drink in its own right.

$13–15 Ⓕ

Maglieri of McLaren Vale Chardonnay 2002

★ ★ ★ ☆

Maglieri is better known for its robust and earthy red wines but it is amazing how often their whites come up in blind tastings. I would never choose a Maglieri chardonnay normally. I just seem to think of them as a red winemaker—and the fact that it's from McLaren Vale doesn't help. But when I taste it without knowing the label, it's good, rich and great value. Prejudice is an ugly thing—open your mind.

$15–17 Ⓕ

McWilliam's Hanwood Semillon Chardonnay 2002

★ ★ ★ ★ ★

The Hanwood wines offer as much bang for your buck in the under-$10 world as any brand in existence and I reckon this blend of semillon and chardonnay is even better than the award-winning Hanwood chardonnay. The semillon gives the wine nice acid and freshness which complements the peachy, rich chardonnay. You can't go past blends of semillon and chardonnay—they're often the best value on the shelf.

$9–11 Ⓜ

McWilliam's Hanwood Verdelho 2002

★ ★ ★ ☆

Not only do the Hanwood wines represent some of the best value under-$10 wines in the country—this, my dear friends, is as good an introduction to verdelho as you will get. This wine has plenty of tropical fruit aromas and flavours and a hint of sweetness that makes it deliciously easy to gulp down. It is important to serve these slightly sweet wines nice and cold so the sweetness is in balance—stick it in the bottom of the esky for twenty minutes.

$9–11 Ⓜ

McWilliam's Margaret River Chardonnay 2002

★ ★ ★ ★ ☆

This wine is like one of the cheap (depending what you call cheap) BMWs. Margaret River chardonnay is a style normally reserved for people who drive those spunky little Z4 roadsters and dine out at fancy restaurants. But here's the McWilliam's treatment: find some excellent fruit from a great region, make a sympathetic and delicious wine and then sell it for about half what it would cost if it came from someone trendy. You see why people like McWilliam's are important?

$17–19 Ⓜ

Miranda High Country Chardonnay 2002

★ ★ ★ ★

This is the second year in a row this wine has featured in these pages and I think the winemakers should be congratulated for modernising the style, pulling back on the oak and turning this into one very good chardonnay. The source for this wine is the hills around the King Valley (hence the High Country moniker) and that cool-climate edge can be tasted on the palate where the acidity is lovely, making this wine crisp and peachy and just dying for some trout from one of the local streams.

$12–14 Ⓕ

Mitchelton Blackwood Park Riesling 2002

★ ★ ★ ★

You can't go past Blackwood Park. This label has been churning out wonderful, blossomy riesling with delicacy and flavour since Andre Agassi played Wimbledon in hot pink spandex. And like him, it will improve with age— it should cellar for up to ten years, maybe more. This year the Blackwood Park range has been expanded to include a chardonnay and cabernet sauvignon and they are both pretty good as well—but the riesling is the original and the best.

$15–17 Ⓛ ꝫ

Molly Morgan Semillon 2001

★ ★ ★ ★

You'll have to read the back label for the story of Molly Morgan, escaped Second Fleet convict, betrayed mistress and fugitive arsonist, but apparently this wine comes from the land she was granted once she'd done her time. Coming in at a leisurely, fresh 10% alcohol it's unlikely to encourage you to start any fires but quite well suited to putting them out. It's perfect as an aperitif, and lots of lovely lemony acidity make it okay for the cellar, too.

$16–18 Ⓛ

Montana Reserve Sauvignon Blanc 2002 NZ

★ ★ ★ ★

Montana is the biggest winery in New Zealand by an impossibly large margin which means they put out some very good wines at all levels of prices, and this Reserve sauvignon blanc is about the same price as most other producers' standard wine. And it is a very typical style, chock full of zesty gooseberry and herbaceous flavours and a bright, tingly finish. Montana, like the rest of New Zealand, had a pretty disastrous 2003 vintage so pick up these wines quick.

$15–17 Ⓜ

Moss Drummond Hill Chardonnay 2001

★ ★ ★ ★

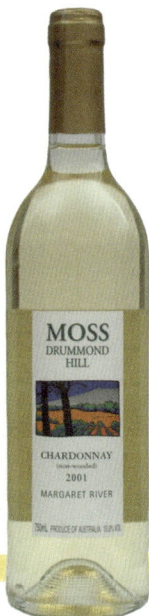

Even though Moss Brothers has been around since 1984, it has always been considered a bit second-tier in the Margaret River region. But the Moss wines have improved out of sight in the past few vintages, while coincidentally a certain Jane Moss has taken the reins of the winery. This chardonnay is very much in the groove for the region. Classical, with notes of cashew, pear and melon, this is a wine that makes you want to love chardonnay all over again.

$15–17 Ⓕ

Moss Drummond Hill Semillon 2002

★ ★ ★ ★ ★

The Moss winery in Margaret River should not be confused with the Moss Wood winery down the road, which also has some jolly nice wines if you're good for an extra thirty bucks a bottle. Moss is becoming an impressive winery in its own right—almost as impressive as the fact that we've managed to review two of their wines without a rolling stone joke—and this semillon, with its citrussy and herby characters is a shining example of their prowess.

$16–18 Ⓛ

Mount Avoca Vineyard Sauvignon Blanc 2002
★ ★ ★ ★

The wines from Mount Avoca have never been really big outside of—well outside of Avoca, to be honest—but they have always included good spicy shiraz and this well-made, tropical sauvignon blanc. The Pyrenees region is a bit of a jack of all trades, seemingly able to ripen all manner of varieties without one really standing out. For what it's worth, though, I think I'll put my money on shiraz and sauvignon blanc.

$16–18 Ⓛ

Mount Pleasant Elizabeth Semillon 1999
★ ★ ★ ★ ★

Are you bored with my annual rave about this wine? I try to be exciting God knows, but it's tough. The Elizabeth has been among the best ten wines for under $20 since the mid 1980s and it shows absolutely no signs of slacking off. It gets a few years longer in the bottle than other whites, it's low in alcohol, has soft, toasty aromas and flavours and it will keep improving for three or four years. Excited? Well just buy it and let's move on.

$16–18 Ⓜ

44 [whites]

O'Leary Walker Adelaide Hills Sauvignon Blanc 2003

★ ★ ★ ★

O'Leary and Walker have waltzed onto the scene in the past couple of years and shown plenty of producers how it should be done. This gorgeously racy, herby, almost flinty sauvignon blanc is the wine you should sit down and drink with prawns all this summer. A wine like this makes me start to question whether our friends from across the pond really do have a monopoly on sauvignon blanc. Look out you Kiwis, we're coming to get you.

$20–22 Ⓛ ⑤

O'Leary Walker Polish Hill River Riesling 2003

★ ★ ★ ★ ★

Both O'Leary and Walker are great winemakers and one of them should take a bow for having made an absolutely pristine, almost centimetre-perfect riesling. Personally I suspect it was Walker at the helm of this one, which is a magical expression of Clare riesling that almost tops the pair's efforts under this label in 2002. Those of us lucky enough to have tasted that wine will know that is high praise indeed.

$20–22 Ⓛ ⑤

O'Leary Walker Watervale Semillon 2002

★ ★ ★ ★

So—just about a clean sweep for the white wines of O'Leary Walker. They make five and we reckon three are sensational. (Actually they're all sensational, we just couldn't review them all. The missing wines are a delicious chardonnay, which sold out before we went to print, and a Watervale riesling which was just edged out by the Polish Hill River.) This Watervale semillon is a lovely wine without the floral and citrus character of riesling or the in-your-face raciness of sauvignon blanc.

$20–22 Ⓛ ⤳

Orlando St Helga Riesling 2002

★ ★ ★ ★

Remember Hagar the Horrible? The well-known and dearly loved cartoon strip? Oh. Well anyway Helga was Hagar's wife and, like her, St Helga is one of those rieslings that keeps trucking on year after year and is as reliable as the daily funnies. St Helga is not at all horrible; she's very nice indeed and has lovely lifted notes of potpourri, some limey intensity on the palate and fine, fresh acid. Eden Valley riesling never looked so good.

$15–17 Ⓛ ⤳

Padthaway Estate
Chardonnay 2002

★ ★ ★ ★

I have said this so many times I'm beginning to bore myself (no mean feat) but just in case this is your first visit to the book I'll say it again: if you want really good-value chardonnay look towards Padthaway. Padthaway Estate is the only label that makes the wines right there in Padthaway—most others ship the fruit to other regions nearby. Another in a long line of well-made chardonnay wines that is almost impossible to fault. Peachy, ripe and well balanced.

$14–16 Ⓕ

Palandri Baldivis Estate
Classic Dry White 2002

★ ★ ★ ☆

Palandri is one of the flashy newcomers to the Margaret River region and one of the largest vineyard owners in Western Australia. A year or two back they bought the Baldivis label and with a few subtle changes the wines seem to be travelling pretty well. Margaret River is home to this style of wine and this is a classic example of the genre, if wine can have a genre. And by the way, after years of mispronouncing this wine I have finally been informed that you say *Bal-dye-vis*.

$13–15 Ⓜ

Penfolds Reserve Bin Semillon 1999

★ ★ ★ ★ ☆

This four-year-old semillon is from the Fleurieu, near McLaren Vale—a long way from the semillon heartlands. It's one of the weirdo experimental wines Penfolds stumbled on in the quest to invent Yattarna, their very pricey flagship white. This is gorgeous, toasty, slightly lemon and honey—and if it were a '99 chardonnay it would either be over the hill or $50 a bottle (or, if it was Yattarna, about double that). So go out and buy some semillon.

$18–20 Ⓜ

Penfolds Thomas Hyland Chardonnay 2002

★ ★ ★ ★

The white wines being made by Australia's most famous red winemaker are improving every day, in fact in some areas outstripping the reds. The new Thomas Hyland range that sits somewhere between the Koonunga Hills and the Bin-series wines is an example—I reckon this lovely, ripe, soft chardonnay is streets ahead of the two Thomas Hyland reds. It's weird because you would expect exactly the opposite; but you know, sometimes the world is just a little bit topsy-turvy—go Penfolds.

$16–18 Ⓜ

Petaluma Hanlin Hill Riesling 2003

★ ★ ★ ★ ☆

Watch out—my wife actually became addicted to this wine last summer and we couldn't have people in our house without her opening a bottle. Of course the 2002 Clare rieslings were sublime, so it was interesting to taste the 2003 and realise it is still pretty damn good, with lots of floral notes and some lovely flinty acidity. As with the 2002 vintage, about half will be bottled under screwcap. Needless to say, buy the screwcap if you can.

$24–26 Ⓛ ⌇

Peter Lehmann Semillon 2002

★ ★ ★ ★ ★

This is the most popular semillon in Australia, which would make it exactly the 181st most popular chardonnay in Australian. And I reckon this is better than the vast majority of those chardonnays so if you want to look a little smarter than the average bear get stuck into this wine. It has lovely lemony aromas and flavours, a soft palate and that all-important 'just drink me you fool' character.

$9–11 Ⓛ

Pierro Semillon Sauvignon Blanc LTC 2003

★ ★ ★ ★

I have long admired this wine as one of the most interesting and complex of the Western Australian SSB styles. I have also loved the fact that when it appears on the table everybody wonders what the LTC stands for and I can tell them it stands for 'Little Touch of Chardonnay', which I also happen to think is extremely cute. This wine is the perfect partner to any Sunday lunch from September to February.

$24–26 Ⓛ ⤳

Poet's Corner Henry Lawson Chardonnay 2001

★ ★ ★ ★ ☆

Calling this the best chardonnay I have ever tasted from Mudgee is a bit like saying I just bumped into the best curling player in Australia—we all know the good ones come from somewhere else. But it must be nice to know you're the big fish, even in a small pond. I will now stop patronising this wine and tell you that it really is delicious—quite restrained, but offering very ripe fruit characters and judicious, not-too-intrusive oak. It's not the best in Australia but it's pretty damn good.

$16–18 Ⓕ

Provenance Pinot Gris 2002

★ ★ ★ ★

I discovered this wine with delight as I made my lazy way down the Great Ocean Road on summer holidays—I don't think I would have tasted it at all had I not gone down that way this year, but it's worth seeking out. It tastes like 'real' pinot gris, by which I mean the stuff that that comes from Germany or Alsace, only not quite as sweet. This is a genuinely interesting wine which shows that this variety might have a spiritual home on the Bellarine Peninsula. Contact the winery direct on 03 5281 7477.

$24–26 Ⓜ

Punt Road Chardonnay 2002

★ ★ ★ ★

The original Punt Road in Melbourne was once described as the product of a planning malfunction, but thankfully it seems not too many things in the winery malfunctioned this vintage. This is Yarra chardonnay with a bit of finesse and a whole lot of honesty, providing all the melony chardonnay characters and some lovely acidity, courtesy of the cool 2002 vintage. Drink it in a traffic jam. If you're in Punt Road you'll have finished the bottle and sobered up before you start moving.

$17–19 Ⓜ

Redbank Sunday Morning Pinot Gris 2003

★ ★ ★ ★

This is one of the first pinots gris that really made me excited (in a positive way, at any rate) and even in a year when the King Valley was hot, dry and close to some nasty bushfires, the quality of the wine still shines. The winemakers and grapegrowers have clearly joined forces to make sure the style stayed true to type. Good silky pinot gris, with fresh acidity—excellent with pasta.

$20–24 Ⓜ

Riddoch Sauvignon Blanc 2002

★ ★ ★ ★ ★

Not renowned for sauvignon blanc, the Coonawarra—it's all about cabernet sauvignon in this region but as this wine goes to show they can turn a nifty, fresh and zesty little white, if you don't mind, just as well. The Riddoch reds have been a staple in lists of the best-value reds from Coonawarra in recent years and this tropical, clean, fruit-driven wine sits well in their company. This is one for those varietal Nazis who think only one variety can grow in any given region.

$16–18 Ⓛ

Rosemount Giants Creek Chardonnay 2002

★ ★ ★ ★

This wonderful wine again shows how the Australian winemakers both big and small (and Rosemount is most definitely big) can tweak their style to match the changing tastes of consumers. Rosemount's cheaper chardonnays are sweet and fruity, and this wine couldn't be further away in style. It is genuinely classy, with well-ripe figgy characters combining with excellent acidity and balance to produce the very model of the modern $20 chardonnay.

$20–22 (F)

Rothbury Brokenback Semillon 2002

★ ★ ★ ★ ☆

This is a good investment I reckon, because it's the sort of wine that has been designed for ageing—quite a bit wouldn't hurt—so buy some and store it somewhere cool and dark. While it is a tight, fine, lemony wine at the moment, by 2006 it will be showing just a hint of toasty development and the colour will be a tiny bit deeper; by 2007, when the wine is five years old, you will really begin to see the magic of aged Hunter semillon.

$22–24 (L)

Salisbury Chardonnay 2002

★ ★ ★ ☆

The Salisbury winery was purchased by West Australian group Evans and Tate in 2002 and the new labels feature a little nod towards their owners in the top corner. Without passing judgment on whether this is a good idea or not, the main thing is that the wine quality has taken a pretty obvious leap in the right direction. This fairly simple, peachy chardonnay won't move any mountains but it is a perfectly good drink at a very fair price.

$9–11 Ⓜ

Saltram Semillon 2002

★ ★ ★ ★ ☆

The 2002 vintage of this wine might still be on the shelves if you look hard enough and I suggest you look pretty hard. For less than $10, this is one of the great white wine buys in Australia. One hundred per cent Barossa semillon, but so racy, grassy and fresh you would swear it came from somewhere cool like Margaret River. The winemakers promise it is all Barossa and that just goes to show what a good, cool vintage can do—buy up this wine, because the 2003 might not be as good.

$9–11 Ⓛ

Sandalford Semillon Sauvignon Blanc 2003

★ ★ ★ ★ ☆

I have always had a soft spot for the wines from Sandalford, and this one sits happily in the upper echelon of the Margaret River style. In its sexy clear bottle the wine looks almost impossibly pale—but also fresh and vibrant, which is exactly how it is, and exactly how it ought to be. It has the grassiness you get from Margaret River semillon combined with gooseberry and melon characters from the sauvignon blanc. And it even has a screwcap—bloody terrific.

$23–25

Seppelt Victorian Chardonnay 2002

★ ★ ★ ★ ★

Seppelt has had yet another facelift and if you don't recognise this wine on the shelf I can't blame you. But it is sure as hell worth seeking out because this is seriously good chardonnay at the price. This wine has some notes of melon and lovely acidity but the best thing about it surely is the daggy name and the daggy label. That just means that the trendies will never buy it and it will never appear on fancy wine lists—so there will be more for you and me.

$12–14 (M)

Seresin Sauvignon Blanc 2003 NZ

★ ★ ★ ★ ★

I love this label and I love this wine. The winemaker has clearly decided that there are enough simple fruity sauvignon blancs around so he's fermented a bit of his in oak and blended in around 10% semillon. The result is a much more complex wine than the vast majority in this style. And what it lacks in instant pungency on the nose, it more than makes up for on the palate. An absolute pearler.

$21–23 Ⓜ

Shadowfax Sauvignon Blanc 2002

★ ★ ★ ★

This grassy little beauty is sourced from the Adelaide Hills and made in the wilds of the African savannah. At least that was where I thought I was when I first visited the Shadowfax winery, which is next to the Werribee Plains Zoo on Melbourne's outskirts. 'The only wine made in close proximity to Mokoko the Hippopotamus,' could be their unique selling proposition. If you happen to visit, take him a bottle of this lovely, lively stuff. It would certainly keep me happy.

$18–20 Ⓛ

Shaw and Smith Sauvignon Blanc 2003

★ ★ ★ ★

Despite a difficult vintage due to the weather and some ill-timed ill health at the winery (get better soon Mr Shaw, you can't let Mr Smith do it on his own!) this wine continues to impress and is now firmly established as the Australian brand leader for the variety. Another example of fresh, lifted, pungent, racy sauvignon blanc, albeit a little less herbaceous than the extraordinary 2002 vintage.

$22–24 Ⓛ

St Hallett Blackwell Semillon 2001

★ ★ ★ ★

I know, people are going to say why doesn't he stop already on the 2002 semillons, surely he knows we are only interested in drinking chardonnay? Semillon is about as fashionable as Pseudo Echo and Barossa semillon is even less cool than the Uncanny X-Men. But these are great wines at great prices and be honest with yourself—if you were just interested in chardonnay would you really have bought this book? Oh, you stole it.

$18–20 Ⓜ

St Huberts Chardonnay 2002

★ ★ ★ ☆

St Huberts has long been a favourite of mine and it is terrific to see them turn out a sophisticated wine like this. It has a little more 'funk' than the average big-company chardonnay, which may be explained by the winemaker experimenting with wild ferments, meaning you add no cultured yeasts, you just let the crazy, feral ones do the job. It's given the wine some exotic nutty and mealy characters, but on a solid base of very good quality, ripe fruit—and more sensible winemaking practices.

$22–24 Ⓕ

Stonehaven Limestone Coast Chardonnay 2001

★ ★ ★ ★

I have not had a bad wine from Stonehaven since it came onto the market a few years back. With the mighty resources of BRL Hardy behind the label the wines always deliver plenty of flavour and character at the price. You can decide for yourself whether you like the frosted bottle; as I am renowned for having no taste or style whatsoever I will not offer my opinion (I hate it). But I like the wine—quite a lot.

$13–15 Ⓜ

Taltarni Fiddleback 2002
★ ★ ★

Once upon a time there was a wine produced in the Pyrenees region of Victoria called Blanc de Pyrenees. Not surprisingly, the bloke responsible for the wine was a Frenchman. So what happens when the Aussies take over? Blanc de Pyrenees turns magically into Fiddleback, which despite sounding a bit like a bad American country rock outfit, is probably a better name to sell wine in this country. The wine remains as good as ever and is ideal for picnics.

$13–15 Ⓛ

Taylors Riesling 2003
★ ★ ★ ★

Taylors riesling, like many from the Clare Valley, is exemplary almost to the point of tedium. I mean there are only so many times you can comment on the lovely lime and floral notes on the nose, the slight hint of sweetness, the fresh acidity on the palate and the fact you love the screwcap so much you have asked it out on a date—several times. This is another one, just like the other ones. An early drinker, however. Don't bother cellaring it, just knock it back with Vietnamese soup sometime soon.

$15–17 Ⓛ ⟆

Tempus Two Semillon Sauvignon Blanc 2003
★ ★ ★ ★ ★

Tempus Two is one of those brands that has got under my radar screen in the past but has now popped up like a B52 with a full payload. Driven by the passionate and fearsomely talented Lisa McGuigan (daughter of Brian) this brand has a strong following in Sydney and will gain fans around the country if they keep making wines like this. A tropical fruit tingle in a glass—this is the perfect summer wine.

$15–17 Ⓜ ⬲

Tim Adams Riesling 2003
★ ★ ★ ★

Tim Adams is a big bear of a man making great, honest, flavoursome, bullshit-free wines in the Clare Valley. This particular riesling is intriguing because it seems so much better than the 2002 vintage, hailed by all and sundry as the vintage of the millennium (I always thought that was a bit of a risky call when you've still got 998 vintages to go). This has terrific acidity and beautiful limey flavours. It's a no-nonsense, just-bloody-drink-it-and-open-another-bottle wine.

$20–22 Ⓛ ⬲

Trentham Estate Viognier 2002

★ ★ ★ ★ ☆

Viognier is the new verdelho. Everyone is talking about it (so it's unfortunate that no one can pronounce it) and they're saying it's the next big thing in white wine. For goodness sake it even had its own symposium last year! The coolest dudes are blending it with shiraz like they do in France, but occasionally you find a really good straight varietal viognier. This has lovely aromas and flavours of apricot and a nice clean finish. (It's *vee-on-yay*, by the way.)

$14–16 Ⓜ

Tyrrell's Moon Mountain Chardonnay 2002

★ ★ ★ ★ ★

This is a truly delicious wine and an absolute steal at the price. What this wine does best is show the doubters just how good Hunter Valley chardonnay can be. In typical Tyrrell's style the wine is quite tight in its youth and with little of the buttery, creamy character of so many other chardonnays. This means I think the wine will mature beautifully for the next three or four years so pick up a few bottles and stash 'em away.

$20–22 Ⓜ

Vasse Felix Classic Dry White 2003
★ ★ ★ ★

Vasse Felix pretty much owns the classic dry white category—with its classic white label and consistently delicious wine I guess it should come as no surprise. You shouldn't worry about drinking a wine like this nice and young—they are at their best racy, vibrant and youthful so you can happily tuck into this new vintage with abandon.

$16–18 Ⓜ

Veritas Christa Rolf Semillon 2002
★ ★ ★ ★ ☆

The Veritas winery is best known for some monumental Barossa reds but you should stop, grab a baguette and some of Maggie Beer's paté and have a taste of this wine. Last year the 2001 vintage of this wine won a couple of trophies at the local Barossa wine show. This one could be even better—the 2002 was a better vintage in the Barossa and at the price, it's very fine drinking indeed. Christa and Rolf are brother and sister and they make the wines together—how sweet!

$14–16 Ⓜ

West Cape Howe Semillon Sauvignon Blanc 2003

★ ★ ★ ☆

On my list of wineries to watch in 2004 is West Cape Howe which, after a couple of years in business, is settling in very nicely down the south west corner of Western Australia. Each wine of theirs I have tasted has had all the right bits in all the right places and this SSB (as we call them in the trade) is a cracker. It has herbaceous and grassy notes and a lovely citrussy palate that makes you want to keep drinking it until the sun goes down.

$20–22 Ⓜ

West Cape Howe Unwooded Chardonnay 2003

★ ★ ★ ☆

All of the West Cape Howe wines impress, even the ones I don't expect to like such as unwooded chardonnay. The fruit comes from the Great Southern area in Western Australia— the most exciting new region in the country for all sorts of varieties including chardonnay. This wine not only has a little more complexity and interest than your average simple peachy unwooded chardonnay, it has nice mouthfeel and length to boot.

$15–17 Ⓜ

Westend Richland Sauvignon Blanc 2003

★ ★ ★ ★ ★   [best value white wine]

They've done it again! The 2002 vintage of this wine was probably the best-value sauvignon blanc in the country but I must admit to thinking it would probably be a one-off thanks to a cool vintage up in the Riverina. But clearly there's a bit of depth to the winemakers at Westend. This year's version is a ripper too, a true varietal expression of sauvignon blanc—grassy and herbaceous, with fresh acid and a bracing tang on the palate—and spectacularly awesome value.

$9–11 Ⓛ ⌇

Wirra Wirra Scrubby Rise Sauvignon Blanc Semillon Viognier 2002

★ ★ ★ ☆

This is a real little fruit bomb that is blissfully uncomplicated and thoroughly delicious—a wine that seems to know just what it needs to be. It needs to be a little bit fruity, a little bit fresh, a little bit tarty and a little bit more than $10. Quite a recipe for success. Mind you, I'm not completely sure about Scrubby Rise as a name for a nice, fresh wine. What is Scrubby rising against—the oppression of the masses?

$14–16 Ⓛ

Wither Hills Chardonnay 2001 NZ

★ ★ ★ ★

Whither Wither Hills? Well wherever it's headed, the winery is currently located in the rather better-known-for-sauvignon-blanc region of Marlborough in New Zealand. But while the Wither sauvignon is pretty good, it is the chardonnay that lifted my shirt and tickled my tummy this year. The Kiwi winemakers love their toys, and this lush, ripe wine has had the full gamut of winemaking bells and whistles thrown at it. But damn, it's lovely.

$22–24 Ⓜ

Wolf Blass Riesling 2003

★ ★ ★ ★

Depending on where you are or when you get down to the shops you might find either the 2002 or 2003 Wolf Blass riesling on the shelf. Personally I wouldn't get too hung up about which one to choose because they're both pretty good, made in that classic Wolf Blass style. There's plenty of juicy fresh fruit characters, a little hint of sweetness and excellent balance. A salutary lesson to any one who doesn't like riesling—defy them not to like this.

$10–12 Ⓛ

Wynns Coonawarra Estate Riesling 2002
★ ★ ★ ★ ★

One of the most consistent wines in the country, this is another maverick example of great Coonawarra white wine. The riesling vines at Wynns must be under some threat because they can surely fetch more bucks per acre from red varieties. But this wine should never be allowed to disappear—a perfectly crafted, softly floral style that gives riesling a great name. If the 2002 is running out you can feel sure that the 2003 will follow along a very well-trodden path.

$12–14 Ⓛ ⤴

Yarra Burn Semillon Sauvignon Blanc 2002
★ ★ ★ ★

This is a delicious, zesty wine that makes me think of lemons and limes and the beauty of Asian food. I think wines like this are our perfect accompaniment to Thai food. They have enough flavour and power not to be overwhelmed by the occasional fiery dish but they also have the right amount of freshness and acidity to keep the palate alive. You should be okay with the 2003 too, although it was a warmer vintage than 2002 and thus it may not have quite as much zip.

$16–18 Ⓜ

Yering Station Chardonnay 2001

★ ★ ★ ★ ★

Yering Station is the new showcase of the Yarra Valley. There's the beautiful old house, the amazing winery, the underground cellars and the fancy restaurant; and the wines fit right in. This chardonnay is a delight, yet another example of the 'new' chardonnay, that doesn't have all that planky wood and over-ripe fruit. Nope, this is elegant and classic and completely lovely.

$20–22 Ⓕ

Zarephath Chardonnay 2002

★ ★ ★ ★

The Benedictine monks who make the Zarephath wines in the Porongurups down in the Great Southern area of Western Australia clearly know a thing or two about making good chardonnay. This is the second vintage of this chardonnay that I have thought is terrific so we can firmly say the Circle of Christ is on a roll.

The wine may be hard to find, so I suggest you call the winery (it may be a little difficult for many readers to pop in) on 08 9853 1152.

$22–24 Ⓕ

Zilzie Buloke Reserve Classic Dry White 2003

★ ★ ★ ★ ★

The Zilzie wines are making quite a name for themselves and here is further proof they are with us for the long haul. A classic dry white is by definition a blend of all sorts and this one is a blend of 'premium varieties', as the Zilzie website coyly notes, among which semillon and sauvignon blanc are certainly prominent.

$10–12 Ⓛ

reds

The big improver in these pages is merlot—the once-maligned merlot that I have in the past sledged with a vigour that would make Glenn McGrath blush. Premium merlot can still be thin and insipid, and nowhere near as good value as similarly priced shiraz. But the less expensive merlots are certainly better than a couple of years ago and I still reckon there are better merlots for under $12 than there are for more than $20.

It remains very difficult to make good pinot noir for under $20 but there are a few crackers for just a few dollars over, so go on—splurge a lobster and a few coins once in a while for a hint of what the pinot noir fuss is about.

Oh, and shiraz and shiraz-based blends still offer the best-value reds in the country by a mile. Simple as that.

Annie's Lane Shiraz 2001

★ ★ ★ ★

Annie's Lane has been turning out some of the best-value red wines from the Clare Valley for seven or eight years now and this 2001 shiraz is no exception—rich and fruity with excellent balance. There is even a small amount bottled under screwcap that I think you can buy direct from the cellar door, so why not pick one up, along with a bottle under cork, and see what all the fuss is about? I've tasted both and while the wine under cork is delicious, the screwcapped one is better.

$16–18 Ⓕ ⤳

Ashwood Grove Cabernet Sauvignon 2002

★ ★ ★

The Ashwood Grove wines have impressed me for a few years now and yet again this wine shows the quality of the 2002 reds from the warm dry inland regions of Australia. This is a cabernet that has clearly been designed with early drinking in mind—it sure ain't one for the cellar, but the quality of the fruit just shines through. This is as gluggable as Gatorade during the City to Surf. I suggest maybe you sip it on your balcony as you watch the fit people pass by—go on, give them a smile!

$10–12 Ⓜ

Ashwood Grove Shiraz 2002

★ ★ ★ ☆

Now under the banner of Kingston Estate, the wines of Ashwood Grove will hopefully get a bit more recogniton, because they have been great value for money for at least five years. This shiraz has some clove-like characters and is medium-bodied at best but it is certainly a pleasant enough wine and will go down a treat at any party where there are discerning drinkers present. And the good thing about bringing along a label no one has heard of is they don't know how much you've spent.

$10–12 Ⓜ

Baileys 1920s Block Shiraz 2001

★ ★ ★ ★

Are you a red-blooded Australian? You will be after a couple of glasses of 1920s Block. This is a rallying call to all those who wish to take arms against a sea of trendies and declare big, gutsy, classic wines like this Glenrowan juggernaut national treasures. Have your local butcher fetch you a large animal and throw it on a spit; maybe you could even sing the national anthem…The Baileys wines are improving fast despite the fact they continue to be ignored.

$20–22 Ⓕ

Balnaves Cabernet Merlot 2000

★ ★ ★ ★

The Balnaves wines are tremendous and anything they do with cabernet sauvignon is okay with me. This wine is lighter in body than the straight cabernet sauvignon, so my counsel to the smart drinkers of Australia would be to drink this one up over the next few years while you wait for the varietal cabernet sauvignon to mature into something really special. If you can't find Balnaves at your favourite store ring the winery on 08 8737 2946 and get put on their mailing list.

$24–26 Ⓜ

Bleasdale Mulberry Tree Cabernet Sauvignon 2001

★ ★ ★ ★

The Bleasdales have been making wonderfully soft, sweet and generous wines from Langhorne Creek for generations and this one is straight from the mould. They have no trouble down in this region getting ripe fruit flavours into their wines and this one smells of mulberry and eucalyptus and the palate is plush and inviting—like a velour lounge in front of the television on a rainy Sunday afternoon.

$16–18 Ⓜ

Blue Pyrenees Shiraz 2001

★ ★ ★ ★

This is a spicy little central Victorian wine that provides an excellent counterpoint to the rich and sweet South Australian styles. The Blue Pyrenees winery changed hands last year after forty years of French ownership and it's now back in the hands of good old Aussie battlers. So if you had been boycotting the wines since the South Pacific Nuclear Testing (who remembers that?) you have the green light to drink them again. Why not start with this one?

$15–17 Ⓜ

Brand's Coonawarra Cabernet Sauvignon 2001

★ ★ ★ ★ ☆

Brand's continues to churn out some of the best-value red wine in Coonawarra. They simply source great fruit from some of the best old vineyards in the region, make the wine carefully with good oak maturation and then they sell it at a price that makes the competition blush. Really I could tell you of a dozen cabernet sauvignon wines at double this price that don't hold a candle to this wine. Will I name them? No, just rest assured none of them is in this book.

$22–24 Ⓕ

{reds}

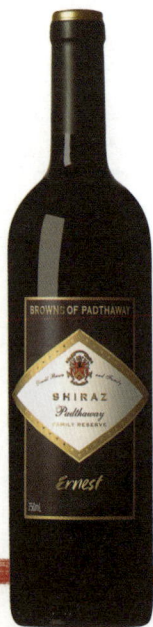

Browns of Padthaway Ernest Shiraz 2001

★ ★ ★ ★

Don't confuse the Browns of Padthaway with the more famous Brown Brothers of Milawa. There are, of course, brothers in the Browns of Padthaway family but no one ever calls them the Brown Brothers because everyone is scared that the ACCC will crash a family gathering and accuse them of passing off. Ernest was a Brown brother and father and the wine after which he is named is a butch, oaky and rich shiraz made from some of the oldest vines in Padthaway.

$17–19 Ⓕ

Cape Schank Pinot Noir 2001

★ ★ ★ ★

The Cape Schank pinot noir comes from the fabulous t'Gallant winery on the Mornington Peninsula, which is best known for its curious obsession with pinot gris and in early 2003 was purchased by Beringer Blass. This pinot noir is a good varietal example of the style, albeit without some of the verve and style of the more expensive pinots from the Peninsula. A terrific introduction to pinot at a very fair price.

$18–20 Ⓛ

Casella Estate Yendah Vale Durif 2001

★ ★ ★ ☆

The Casella family has struck gold in recent years with the release of a brand called Yellowtail that has become the most popular Australian wine in the US without ever having been released here. So while they send their massive volumes to the States we get to have a taste of some of Casella's more interesting wines, like this durif—a big, mouthfilling mongrel of a wine that you should consume with a brontosaurus steak. If you like 'em big and dry, look no further.

$16–18 Ⓕ

Casella Estate Yendah Vale Tempranillo 2001

★ ★ ★

I'm not sure whether the wine or the name is a bigger mouthful but this is definitely a wine worth seeking out. We are seeing a little more tempranillo, which is the variety that makes Spain's famous Rioja wines, in Australia and this is one of the better examples. The wine is rich and full bodied with some intriguing savoury characters and some drying tannin. Worth a try next time you have your Spanish friends around for some tapas.

$16–18 Ⓕ

{reds}

Charles Melton Rose of Virginia 2003

★ ★ ★ ★

This is always one of our favourite pink wines and the 2003 treads a well-worn track. It's a bright, gorgeous magenta colour and has lovely cherry and raspberry aromas and flavours and just a hint of sweetness to make it go down nice and easy. When do you drink rosé? My suggestions are: at lunch in spring, at a picnic with antipasta, playing lawn bowls or when it's too hot to drink red wine and you've run out of white. Remember to chill it well.

$17–19 Ⓛ 🍦

Cheviot Bridge Yea Valley Shiraz 2001

★ ★ ★ ★

Here is a wine not trying to be anything it isn't. It is fairly subtle, medium-bodied shiraz sourced from Yea, which is kind of in the middle of nowhere. It is no full-bodied blockbuster and the tannins are fine and soft. Which might not make it sound like the most interesting wine, but if they held a race to finish a bottle of shiraz at lunchtime tomorrow, this would most likely be the empty bottle in my hand as I staggered across the finish line.

$24–26 Ⓜ

D'Arenberg d'Arry's Original Shiraz Grenache 2001

★ ★ ★ ★ ★

Utilising fruit sourced from McLaren Vale, this is a serious wine for serious wine lovers. More than once, however, I've seen it priced closer to $15 than $20 which makes it a bargain like no other—and if you are used to drinking $10 wines, this will show you what a few extra bucks can get you. Here you have earthy, spicy characters, a lovely core of sweet grenache fruit and genuine weight and complexity on the palate. If you see it close to $15, buy as much as you can afford.

$18–20 Ⓕ

De Bortoli Sacred Hill Cabernet Merlot 2002

★ ★ ★ ★ ★

Light bodied, a little bit plummy, not at all tarty and horrible like so many cheap reds, and $6. Yes, that's right: $6—maybe less. I don't know how they do it, but De Bortoli have got the recipe right at the moment. This should be the standby wine, the wine you have a case of in case the family drops in. I mean there aren't that many people you'd begrudge spending six bucks on are there? Well yes, I can think of a few too, now you mention it.

$6–8 Ⓛ

De Bortoli Gulf Station Pinot Noir 2002

★ ★ ★ ★

This is the wine I use when explaining to a class of novice wine drinkers what inexpensive pinot noir should taste like. Sure, it is a bit strawberry-like and doesn't have great weight on the palate; but it does show some pointers towards what good pinot noir can be. The problem with pinot noir is that yields in the vineyard must be very low for the fruit to be really good and when yields are low prices must go up. Therefore: not much good cheap pinot—this is the best of a bad bunch.

$16–18 Ⓛ

Deakin Estate Cabernet Sauvignon 2001

★ ★ ★ ★ ★

The Deakin Estate wines were very good when they first appeared a decade ago, but I guess I haven't been paying attention lately—the quality of this cabernet really caught me by surprise (although I don't suppose it's the first Deakin to have caught a parishioner by surprise). It has lovely soft, light cherry and plum flavours and a well-balanced finish. Try it with lamb.

$10–12 Ⓜ

Elderton Shiraz 2001
★ ★ ★ ★

Elderton is a Barossa stalwart, peopled by some fine folk and with a loyal customer base who think that the sun shines out of Elderton's pants. Well the sun certainly shone on the shiraz vines in 2001 because this is a big, rich wine with loads of ripe fruit characters and mercifully not as much oak as the old days. Certainly there is a lick of vanilla oak but it's the fruit that steals the show here—rich and hearty and perfect for a thick steak.

$26–28 Ⓕ

Ferngrove Estate Dragon Shiraz 2001
★ ★ ★ ★

My first visit to Frankland River in 2003 impressed upon me what a great region it will become for shiraz, and I reckon it's made a flying start. This is a wine for the cellar. At the moment it has some smoky notes on the nose and an intense, rich palate with notably robust tannins, but time will tame it nicely. The Dragon, incidentally, is the name of an orchid that grows locally and is unique to the region. And I reckon you'll be breathing fire too after a bottle of this.

$23–25 Ⓕ

{reds} 79

Ferngrove Estate Merlot 2001

★ ★ ★ ★

Ferngrove is a relatively new winery in Western Australia's Frankland River region and it has racked up a few gold medals and trophies in its short lifetime. This merlot is a smooth, soft, well-balanced little number which will be no surprise to those people who think all merlots are soft and smooth, but in fact only the good ones are. With aromas and flavours of blueberries and plum, this is a satisfying drink that slips down perhaps a little too easily.

$14–16 Ⓜ

Fox Creek Shadow's Run Shiraz Cabernet Sauvignon 2001

★ ★ ★ ★ ☆

I have heard people call into question the sanity of the Fox Creek folks for putting their winery dog, Shadow, on the front label of this wine. Why not, I say. Plenty of much sillier things have appeared on wine labels. And the wine Shadow calls his own is a very tasty, rich and solid shiraz cabernet with subtle nuances of friendly dog with its tongue hanging out. Seriously, this is a very good wine, bravely and correctly bottled under screwcap.

$14–16 Ⓕ 🖎

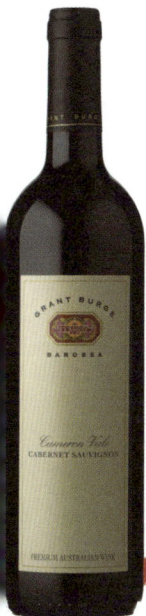

Grant Burge Cameron Vale Cabernet Sauvignon 2001

★ ★ ★ ★

Burgey just keeps on keeping on with a string of good wines now falling under his ever-expanding banner. It is hard to fault any of the Grant Burge wines and this is another well-made, delicious wine that you would be hard pressed not to like. Of course you might not like it if you don't like red wine or if Grant Burge once ran over your cat; but I'm sure Grant's a very careful driver and if you don't like red wine—what are you doing in my book?

$23–25 Ⓕ

Grant Burge Hillcot Merlot 2001

★ ★ ★ ★ ★

The best thing about this Barossa merlot is that it actually tastes like merlot. And what is that? Well it should smell like violets and taste like plums and this wine goes as close as any in this country to getting it right. The wine is rich and soft, which merlot also should be, and even though I can be a bit tough on merlot, this is certainly a wine I could sit down to and sip for quite a while—high praise indeed.

$15–17 Ⓜ

Grant Burge Miamba Shiraz 2001

★ ★ ★ ★

People might start to think that I have a bit of a thing for Grant Burge—it does seem that an extraordinary number of his wines have found their way into these pages, but then he does produce an extraordinary number of good wines. This Miamba shiraz sits between Burge's Barossa Vines shiraz at $15 and his Filsell shiraz at $30, and it sits there very nicely. There are hints of plums and vanilla on the nose, a soft palate with just a hint of tannin and a well-balanced finish.

$20–22 Ⓕ

Hardys Oomoo Shiraz 2001

★ ★ ★ ★

Hardys has released this wine and this label as a tribute to their 150 years in the wine business. The label is a replica of something from the mid-nineteenth century and I have showed it to a few people who think that's where it should have stayed. So it will come as no surprise that I think this label is rather nice—it has a real sense of character. And so does the wine. Good rich, honest and sweet McLaren Vale shiraz with all the right bits in all the right places.

$13–15 Ⓕ

Haselgrove McLaren Vale Shiraz 2002

★ ★ ★

Haselgrove has gone through tumultuous times in the past few years. When the wine sector got over-excited a few years back and everyone was racing in to buy up wineries Haselgrove's buyer, Barrington Estates, went under so the banks ended up owning the place. But this is a terrific wine and hopefully Haselgrove will emerge from this strife intact. Buy the wine and help out a winery that sure as hell needs it.

$16–18 Ⓕ

Hazard Hill Shiraz Grenache 2001

★ ★ ★ ★

This wine comes from the very talented winemakers at Plantagenet in Western Australia and, hello doctor, it's a top little wine at a ripsnorting price. Plenty of juicy fruit character, some nice spice and much more depth than you might expect from a $10 wine. I like it because it's also a little bit weird—I mean shiraz grenache blends really should come from McLaren Vale and the Barossa, not Western Australia. Nothing like having your prejudices challenged.

$10–12 Ⓜ

Hewitson Miss Harry Grenache Shiraz Mourvedre 2002
★ ★ ★ ★ ★

It would be far too easy for me to start this review with 'I'm just wild about Harry'. If people are going to pay good money for a wine guide, or even take the trouble to remove it from the recycling bin, they deserve better than that. So I will talk about the intense raspberry and dark fruit character of this wine, its lovely medium-bodied mouthfeel, its good structure and its utter drinkability. And I will tell you that winemaker Dean Hewitson might be the cousin of celebrity chef Iain.

$22–24 Ⓜ

Houghton Crofters Shiraz 2001
★ ★ ★ ★ ★

The Westie winemakers at Houghton are cranking out some of the best wine in the country, and here is another example. This isn't one of those fresh and fruity styles; this is a 'serious' wine with structure and complex flavours, a wine that might almost be a lot more expensive. It is still a bit closed and tight but will evolve beautifully over the next five years.

$23–25 Ⓜ

Hugo Shiraz 2001
★ ★ ★

The Hugo wines remind me of a different time, particularly this shiraz. It reminds me of a time when Aussie reds were chock full of American oak and smelled a bit like Bounty bars or Reef Oil. The oak used to give shiraz a coconut smell and this wine still has a whiff of it, which is not entirely a bad thing because the wine also has some good, ripe fruit flavours. It won't blow your mind but it will take you back to a time when you wore shoulder pads and thought Simon Le Bon was a sex god.

$18–20 Ⓕ

Ingoldby Shiraz 2001
★ ★ ★ ★ ☆

The Ingoldby wines impress right across the board and are very much in the style that should shut those people up (well all right they're mostly blokes) who complain that you can't get any decent, full-bodied reds for $10 anymore. Well here's one: packed with generous McLaren Vale shiraz fruit and only a whiff of new oak, and with some real grunt on the palate. This is a classic Aussie red—show it to your overseas mates.

$13–15 Ⓕ

Jacob's Creek Reserve Shiraz 2001

★ ★ ★ ★ ☆

The brands of Southcorp hit a few troubles this year but Jacob's Creek just seems to go from strength to strength. Could it be that they have simply stuck to doing exactly what made them good in the first place—making good wines for great prices and never letting their standards slip? The Reserve wines follow exactly the same recipe and what do you know, they're a smash hit. This wine is richly flavoured, generously oaked and full bodied to boot.

$15–17 Ⓕ

Jamiesons Run Coonawarra Cabernet Sauvignon 2001

★ ★ ★ ★

One of a stable of terrific new varietal wines from Jamiesons Run, this was a winner at the Sydney Wine Show as the best under-$20 red. We don't think it's quite *that* good, but it certainly is a well-made style that won't disappoint any drinkers looking for honest flavour and value. There is a touch of mintiness, some real cherry flavours and only a subtle hint of oak. This is the first release and it's pretty good gear; but first releases are always good, aren't they?

$16–18 Ⓕ

Jamiesons Run Coonawarra Shiraz 2001

★ ★ ★ ★ ★

There are now more versions of Jamiesons Run than there were sequels to *Police Academy*, which makes me wonder about the health of the original Jamiesons Run blend. Quite simply, this wine and the cab sav are so good, I wonder if they have enough fruit to keep the original blend up to its old standard. But let me and the winemakers worry about that—you should just drink this spicy and soft shiraz and enjoy.

$16–18 Ⓜ

Kangarilla Road Shiraz 2001

★ ★ ★ ★ ☆

Kangarilla Road makes some of the most consistently good-value red wines in McLaren Vale. Every year their cabernet sauvignon and shiraz come out and look rich, intense, well balanced and regional in that big, soft McLaren Vale way. The shiraz features here simply because it won the toss over the cabernet sauvignon. It's not always easy to get, however, so I suggest you give the winery a call to find out if there is a retail stockist near you—08 8383 0533.

$22–24 Ⓕ

[reds] 87

Kingston Merlot 2002

★ ★ ★

They used to market this as the wine that allowed you to 'bend the rules', which meant it was a red wine you could drink with fish or some other out-there type of food. My thinking is: who in their right mind would care? There are already quite enough rules on this earth without applying them at the dinner table. So this plummy, soft merlot can be drunk with whatever the bloody hell you like—chocolate cake, kebabs or artichoke puree—go for broke.

$12–14 Ⓛ

Kirrihill Clare Valley Shiraz 2001

★ ★ ★ ★

This wine is terrific value and a lesson in marketing for new players. Kirrihill have ticked all the boxes: they employed a well-regarded winemaker, they stuck to the best varieties that the Clare could offer and they priced their wines sensibly so people would be willing to take a punt on them. This is the model of modern Clare shiraz—a hint of blueberry and mint on the nose, some judicious and generous oak handling and a big, rich, tasty palate.

$20–22 Ⓕ

Leasingham Bastion Shiraz Cabernet 2001

★ ★ ★ ★ ☆

The Bastion came onto the market with one of the great red wine bargains of the decade—that 1999 vintage was something very special. The 2000 was pretty good too but not great, and if they hadn't come up with the goods for the 2001 we might have all thought it was a con. It ain't no con—the 2001 Bastion is back up there, close to the 1999 vintage as a crackerjack wine at a crazy price. I have already seen this wine hovering around the $10 mark; if you see it there, pounce.

$12–14 Ⓕ

Leconfield Cabernet Sauvignon 2001

★ ★ ★ ★

When this wine popped up as one of our best reds in a blind tasting, my eyebrows were raised somewhat because in the past I've found Leconfield reds too 'leafy'—meaning the fruit hasn't tasted quite ripe. Someone at the winery must have agreed because this 2001 vintage is a significant change in the house style. It's riper and better balanced and tastes much more like a classic Coonawarra red. So good on Leconfield—with wines like this, I could get to like them.

$28–30 Ⓕ

Lillydale Estate Pinot Noir 2001

★ ★ ★ ★

Lillydale Estate is part of the McWilliam's empire so it's not surprising that it does the McWilliam's thing: it's a terrific example of a regional style, in this case Yarra Valley pinot noir, at a very fair price. The wine has lovely aromas of strawberry and some smoky oak, and the palate is smooth and long with unexpected complexity. There's also some of that lovely silky, sexy pinot character that you get in the really expensive ones.

$23–25 Ⓛ

Maglieri of McLaren Vale Cabernet Sauvignon 2001

★ ★ ★ ★ ★

Maglieri was bought by Beringer Blass a few years ago, and it's now not as trendy as it used to be, but the wine has shown no sign of dropping in quality. This is gutsy and full-blooded cabernet, not a soft, thin wine but an old-fashioned Aussie style with a heart of gold and the odd rough edge. Jeez, I'm starting to sound like Barnesy (I would not, however, go as far as to say this wine's got blue denim in its veins).

$17–19 Ⓕ

Maglieri of McLaren Vale Shiraz 2001

★ ★ ★ ★

I was a bit disappointed in some of the McLaren Vale reds from 2000. It clearly wasn't a crash hot vintage and my suggestion to you is to stick to the vintages either side, 1999 or 2001, both of which were much better than the Millennium vintage. This 2001 shiraz is another example—the Maglieri red wines from McLaren Vale are definitely hitting their straps and this is rich and round, with more depth than the 2000 vintage. It'll cellar for a few years to boot.

$17–19 Ⓕ

Margan Merlot 2002

★ ★ ★ ☆

There is not a dud in the entire Margan range; even their merlot is good. Now I must declare my interest here because apparently my old man used to play golf with old man Margan (although I've never met him myself). So I asked my old man what Mr Margan was like as a golfer and his blunt response was, 'Should stick to wine.' And so with no further comment on Mr Margan's backswing I recommend you try his excellent merlot—soft, with cherry flavours, and very smooth.

$19–21 Ⓜ

Margan Shiraz 2002

★ ★ ★ ☆

I reckon a few more of the Hunter Valley's winemakers could take a trip to Margan to see how you produce excellent wine at good prices. One tip: the wines are always released early so the business can get cashflow. Consequently I recommend you leave this wine in the cellar for a bit to let it acquire some more character than the simple juicy fruit you get at the moment. There's earthiness and a hint of spice, and in a year or two this will be terrific with a chargrilled steak.

$19–21 Ⓜ

McWilliam's Hanwood Merlot 2002

★ ★ ★ ★ ☆

The merlot grapes that came out of the Riverina in 2002 could well be the best ever for the region and thus it is no surprise that McWilliam's got its hands on some good gear. This wine shows lovely soft, plum and cherry characters and is light to medium bodied—perfect for someone who doesn't really like big, bold reds with body and tannin. And that is the way cheap merlot should be— a bit of a Claytons red, the one you have when you're not having a red.

$9–11 Ⓜ

Meerea Park Shiraz Viognier 2002

★ ★ ★

Shiraz viognier blends are the winemaking equivalent of ugg boots at the moment—big with the groovers, while the rest of us sit back and wonder what all the fuss is about. This wine from Meerea Park has a dash of (white) viognier—8%—added to the (red, as usual) shiraz and the result is a funky red wine with plenty of interest and character. The viognier is supposed to make the wine more aromatic, and also a little softer. In this case, it works.

$18–20 Ⓜ 🔄

Miranda Mirrool Creek Cabernet Shiraz 2002

★ ★ ★ ★

Miranda go about their business cheerfully, making pretty good wines at pretty good prices—and any winery that makes Passion Pop is all right with me. They may never gain great kudos while Passion Pop still exists (it's *huge* by the way) but wines like the Mirrool Creek red are honest, flavoursome and really good value. 2002 was good for the red varieties around the Riverina, and this wine has more bang than you might expect for the buck.

$10–12 Ⓜ

{reds} 93

Miranda White Shiraz 2002

★ ★ ★ ☆

If we all lived in America this would be the sort of wine we'd see a lot more often. This is modelled on white zinfandel, which is a sweet, pink drink made by pressing the skins off the juice very early in fermentation so as to extract only a little bit of pink colour. Leave a bit of sugar in the wine and Sam's your uncle: America's best seller. It's never really caught on over here—I wonder why? Taste this wine and make up your own mind— I think it's rather delicious in a bubblegum sort of way.

$12–14 Ⓛ 🍷

Mitchell of Clare Grenache 2001

★ ★ ★ ★ ☆

The Mitchell family in Clare has been making the region's best grenache for some time now and this vintage is as good as they have ever done. The wine has those classic raspberry and sweet fruit grenache characters, that lovely bright colour and that whopping lick of alcohol that combine to make you weak at the knees. While I'm not by nature a great fan of grenache on its own, this wine could almost turn me. (I said almost.)

$17–19 Ⓕ 🐍

Montana Reserve Pinot Noir 2001 NZ

★ ★ ★ ★

The Marlborough region is best known for sauvignon blanc but my prediction is that, in time, its pinot noir might become pretty big as well. Since the good folk at Montana are the biggest makers of both varieties in New Zealand, they have a head start. The advantage New Zealand pinots seem to have over the Australian versions is the lovely aromatic character they get, and the winemakers are very sensitive to pinot's vagaries. They make fine, supple wines without any aggressive tannins—like this one.

$18–20 Ⓜ

Moondah Brook Cabernet Sauvignon 2001

★ ★ ★ ★ ☆

The red wines from the Hardys stable in Western Australia just seem to get better and better. The Moondah Brook wines use fruit from Margaret River, the Swan Valley and down in the Great Southern. The result is a fairly elegant representation of WA cabernet sauvignon that is hard not to love. All the flavours of blackcurrant are there and there is only a hint of toasty oak, which makes this not too tough on the palate. Great value.

$15–17 Ⓕ

Nugan Estate Manuka Grove Durif 2001
★ ★ ★ ★

Durif seems to have found its natual home around the Riverina in NSW. It's a big rustic grape variety that the French do not regard highly—they think it's a bit coarse, which they probably think of most Australians as well. But durif can be delicious in a no-holds-barred, full-throttle sort of way. This one is definitely not for wimps—it has great flavours of dark chocolate and brandied cherries and the tannin is well integrated, not chunky like it can be with some other durifs. A good alternative to full-bodied shiraz.

$19–21 Ⓕ

Orlando Russet Ridge Cabernet Shiraz Merlot 1998
★ ★ ★ ★ ☆

I find it almost impossible to believe that a wine as good as this, and from as good a vintage as this, is still sitting around on the shelves. A classic 1998 Coonawarra red blend with some excellent bottle age for less than $15? You have to be joking! But apparently not, because it was certainly available when we went to print and as such it marks one of the great red wine bargains in ages. Just get out there quick and snap this one up—surely it can't last much longer.

$14–16 Ⓜ

Palandri Merlot 2001

★ ★ ★ ☆

Palandri is one of the biggest new wineries in Western Australia and after an initial period where it seemed all that mattered was advertising and throwing functions, they have settled down to concentrate on making some good wine. And this is what Margaret River merlot should taste like, nice and ripe with red berry flavours on the palate, not-too-obvious oak and a nice easy finish that makes you want to throw a function for friends. 'Hey get over here and try some of this merlot.'

$24–26 Ⓜ

Penfolds Rawson's Retreat Shiraz Cabernet 2002

★ ★ ★ ★

I can remember the first time I tasted this wine—I was in Qantas economy class and it was in a little 187 mL screwcap bottle. I think it partnered one of those new-wave airline meals magnificently designed by some famous Australian chef to resemble all the old-wave airline meals and I kept thinking to myself, crikey that's a nice wine. So I had another small bottle just to be sure and before you could say Rawson's Retreat, I was crying over a Hugh Grant/Sandra Bullock movie. The power of wine.

$8–10 Ⓜ

{reds} 97

Peter Lehmann Barossa Shiraz 2001

★ ★ ★ ★ ☆

This wine, along with its maker, should be sanctified. If people ask me what Barossa shiraz tastes like I just point them towards Peter Lehmann— the quintessential taste of Barossa. Rich and sweet with a hint of chocolate and some Christmas cake aromas—this is a beauty. The only thing better than this might well be the 2002 vintage of the same wine which will be available in early 2004. I'd grab some quick. The whisper is it could be awesome.

$18–20 Ⓕ

Peter Lehmann Clancy's Red 2001

★ ★ ★ ★

This blend of shiraz, cabernet sauvignon, cabernet franc and merlot is a classic example of the winemaking art of blending across varieties to get a whole that is greater than the sum of its parts. It's fair to assume that the components in this wine didn't make the cut for the higher-priced wines and would not on their own offer an outstanding drink. But by blending them you get a wholly satisfying wine that will impress anyone who likes it rich and soft.

$15–17 Ⓕ

Pizzini Sangiovese 2001

★ ★ ★ ★ ☆

Fred Pizzini and his family continue to make some of the most exciting wines in Victoria's King Valley, but I still like this one the best. It is very savoury and earthy with a medium-bodied palate and quite drying tannin. While that may not sound so appealing for those of you used to rich, sweet fruit, I implore you to open a bottle of this with your best pasta and see it come alive. Remember all wine should taste better accompanied by food. Some don't—this does.

$22–24 Ⓜ

Plantagenet Omrah Shiraz 2001

★ ★ ★ ★

The Omrah is the second label at Plantagenet but I reckon it's every bit as good as a few 'top' labels. All the Plantagenet reds, from the cheap and cheery Hazard Hill through to the super-posh flagship shiraz, are on song at the moment. This middle sibling has hints of spice and cool-climate pepper combining with some cherry-like flavours to craft a very very nice modern Aussie shiraz. It's made with not much oak at all—and that's a good thing.

$22–25 Ⓜ

{reds}

Primo Estate Shiraz Sangiovese (Il Briccone) 2001

★ ★ ★ ★

Primo Estate is one of those wineries you want to see succeed. They are located in the daggiest region in Australia, the Adelaide Plains, and the bloke behind the label, Joe Grilli, is as nice a guy as you're likely to meet. So when I tell you this blend of Italy's most popular red grape, sangiovese, and our own shiraz is damn good drinking, you should go straight out and buy a case. Don't do it for me—do it for Italian–Australian relations.

$14–16 Ⓜ

Red Hill Estate Pinot Noir 2000

★ ★ ★ ★ ☆

Red Hill on the Mornington Peninsula has one of the most spectacular winery sites of any in Australia with views from Westernport Bay across to Port Phillip. So the vines must have a lovely view—but can they turn out decent wine? Well, a contented vine is obviously a good vine and the pinot noir from Red Hill, while not in the very top echelon of Mornington pinot, is great value with some real varietal definition.

$20–22 Ⓛ

Richmond Grove Limited Release Barossa Shiraz 2000

★ ★ ★ ★ ★

If this wine tasted any more like the Barossa, there would be an oom-pah band and a slice of *bienenstich* in the glass. I tasted this wine with three other people and the only word we all wrote in common was 'Barossa'. The wine has sweet oak characters, plenty of chocolate and vanilla on the nose and the palate is big, rich and soft. You drink a glass and you want to go straight to the Barossa and kiss the soil. Or perhaps that's just me.

$16–18 Ⓕ

Rosemount Hill of Gold Cabernet Sauvignon 2001

★ ★ ★ ★

The Hill of Gold wines are very good indeed, showcasing the versatility of the Mudgee region for good cabernet, shiraz and chardonnay. The cabernet is my pick just because I've realised that I am stuffing this book full of shiraz as I do most years. No, this is a lovely ripe cabernet with some tobacco and earthy flavours as well as the expected spectrum of sweet berry fruits, and with a couple of years in the cellar, I reckon it will develop lovely secondary characters.

$18–20 Ⓕ

Rosemount Shiraz Cabernet Sauvignon 2002

★ ★ ★ ☆

Rosemount's early release reds have always been terrific wines—bright and fruity and disarmingly soft for reds that are sometimes only six months old. It has to do with a clever trick called micro-oxygenation, which essentially means the winemakers can oxygenate the wine to make it softer in its youth when it hits the shelves. This is a plummy, simple, easy-drinking red that just begs for your best spaghetti bolognese.

$10–12 Ⓛ

Rothbury Estate Hunter Valley Shiraz 2001

★ ★ ★ ★

The Rothbury Estate renaissance continues apace under the guidance of the 'other' McGuigan, Neil— brother of Brian, who controls the rapidly growing McGuigan Simeon empire while Neil runs the rather more modest Rothbury Estate, which sits slap-bang in the middle of the Hunter. After a few years in the wilderness the new wines are shining like bright beacons. This is a spicy, very well-made, plummy shiraz with a little hint of that Hunter dirt that we all love.

$14–16 Ⓜ

Rothbury Estate Mudgee Cabernet Merlot 2001

★ ★ ★ ☆

Here's a wine that does Mudgee proud. A modern blend of cabernet sauvignon and merlot from well-established vines at the heart of the region. Aromas of blackcurrant and a hint of spice make you think that this wine would be just the thing for a roast dinner at someone's farm in Mudgee. If you've never been to Mudgee, go—it's a tremendous place and quite beautiful.

$14–16 Ⓜ

Salisbury Shiraz Cabernet Sauvignon 2002

★ ★ ★ ★ ★

When we tasted the red blends this year and then had a look at the winners one thing became blindingly obvious—all the best wines were from 2002 and they were all sourced from the Riverina in NSW. Now for one of these wines to be chosen as a five-star wine might be considered a blip but when three of them get in it's definitely a signal from above. A tasty, well-made red wine with a nice little bit of spice.

$9–11 Ⓜ

Saltram Barossa Shiraz 2002

★ ★ ★ ★ ☆

The Saltram Barossa range only appeared in early 2003 and it shows how much good shiraz they must have had spare at the winery, because this one's a belter. I tasted the 2001 version not so long ago and it was a ripper— then just as I was about to write the review, the 2002 popped up before my very eyes. And it's just as good as the first one: rich, generous and surprisingly soft, it could nevertheless do with a year or so to settle down before you tuck in.

$16–18 Ⓕ

Seppelt Victorian Shiraz 2000

★ ★ ★ ★ ☆

The Seppelt renaissance is a thing of true beauty. If you cast your mind back a few years you will remember Seppelt had labels that more closely resembled Cadbury's Roses than wine, and it's little wonder people went looking elsewhere.

So it is great to see a wonderful old brand, with a real home and a real sense of history, get some of that back into the bottle and onto the label. This is a terrific wine, with juicy, soft shiraz characters, just the faintest whiff of oak and a certain indefinable style.

$13–15 Ⓜ

Sevenhill Shiraz 2000

★ ★ ★ ★

Brother John May must surely be the best Jesuit winemaker in the world. Not to disparage any of those winemaking Jesuits in France and Italy (if there even are any), but the Sevenhill winery in Clare should be a national treasure. The shiraz is the greatest wine that Sevenhill makes and don't think for a second this is some kind of novelty wine because it's made by priests—this is a beautifully made, rich, intense shiraz that sits proudly among the Clare's best.

$24–26 Ⓕ

Seville Estate Pinot Noir 2001

★ ★ ★ ★

Seville Estate is a bit off the beaten track, tucked away in a corner of red Yarra Valley dirt too many miles off the main road to see the tourist traffic that helps other wineries get their names well known. But Seville has been around for more than thirty years and makes some of the best wines in the region. The red soil is perfect for the red varieties and Seville would make one of the best shirazes in the region as well as this fabulously silky pinot noir.

$24–26 Ⓛ

Shane Warne Collection Cabernet Merlot Petit Verdot 2002

★ ★ ★ ★

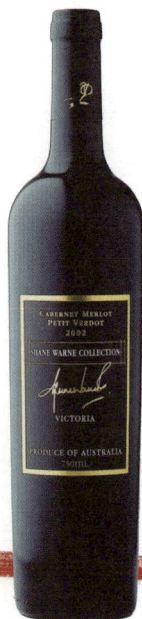

The first vintage of the Shane Warne Collection red was a real humdinger. No surprise the fruit came from a collection of vineyards around Mildura and the wine was made by the team at Zilzie who have so impressed us these past two years. Of course Warney himself didn't have the greatest year in 2003 but his wine seems to be maturing nicely and, just like its namesake, will probably be even better in 2004 after a bit of a rest.

$12–15 Ⓜ

St Hallett Grenache Shiraz Touriga 2002

★ ★ ★ ★ ☆

Although this has been christened the GST, I can tell you it's a damn sight more palatable than any tax. This wine is a kind of turbo version of St Hallett's Gamekeepers Reserve and it has real character and oomph, as most of the wines do from this great Barossa stalwart. Normally with a blend of a grenache and shiraz you would see mourvedre as the third element but the touriga, which is a native Portugese variety used to make port, handles itself with aplomb.

$20–22 Ⓕ

Stepping Stone Coonawarra Cabernet Sauvignon 2001

★ ★ ★ ★ ☆

The Stepping Stone wines come from BRL Hardy and this Coonawarra cabernet sauvignon is another example of what the big boys, with their massive economies of scale, can do when they put their minds to it. The '01 hasn't quite sustained the five-and-a-half-star buzz created by the inaugural 2000 model; but even so a wine like this selling for $12 must put the fear of god into some of the boutique winemakers down in Coonawarra— they simply can't do it for the price.

$12–14 Ⓕ

Sticks Pinot Noir 2002

★ ★ ★ ★

With fruit sourced from the heart of the Yarra Valley, this wine is very close to being the best pinot noir around the traps for less than $20. It is quite an achievement to make a pinot that doesn't just taste thin and insipid at this price. But 'Sticks' Dolan is a clever man (never thought I'd say that about a former Port Adelaide ruckman) and this wine should be your first training-wheels pinot noir before you go out and blow your budget on the posh stuff.

$16–18 Ⓛ

{reds} 107

Tamar Ridge Pinot Noir 2002
★ ★ ★ ★

The Tamar Ridge winery is fast becoming the biggest in Tasmania and its cool-climate wines (particularly pinot and riesling) are taking their place on the tables of the fanciest restaurants on the mainland. This pinot noir is a terrific example of what Tamar does well—get real varietal character into the bottle without too much intrusive oak. If you are in Launceston it would certainly be worth visiting the winery for a look into the future of winemaking in Tassie.

$22–24 Ⓛ

Tatachilla Partners Cabernet Shiraz 2002
★ ★ ★ ★

The winemakers at Tatachilla continue to make excellent wines across the full spectrum of varieties and price points, and The Partners is no exception. The classic blend of cabernet sauvignon and shiraz has been crafted to impress the drinkers of Australia and by golly doesn't it do its job. Nowhere else in the world do they blend these two varieties so can be sure you are doing it for your country when you drink a wine like this. With plenty of honest flavour and richness this is the Aussie barbecue red wine without peer.

$13–15 Ⓜ

Taylors Cabernet Sauvignon 2001

★ ★ ★ ★ ☆

Taylors say this is the best-selling 'premium' cabernet sauvignon in Australia, which is a pretty impressive claim; more impressive still is that they had the guts to whack a few thousand bottles under screwcap. The wine itself is lovely—very forward and fruity with a real attack on the front of the palate. It may not offer the complexity of some others but at the price it is a special—see if you can find the screwcap version and put it in the cellar for a spell.

$15–17 Ⓕ 🍃

Taylors Shiraz 2002
★ ★ ★ ★ ★

The Taylors reds, with their steadfastly mundane (or is that 'classic'?) labels have long had a reputation for good-value drinkability, but they have improved out of sight under the guiding hand of the eccentric but adorable Adam Eggins. Eggins reminds me a bit of a mad scientist—he was dux of the renowned Roseworthy winemaking school and he is forever fossicking and probing, trying to find ways to continually improve his wines. The proof of his success is in the bottle—a big five yums on the Gregorometer for this one.

$17–19 Ⓕ

Tyrrell's Rufus Stone McLaren Vale Merlot 2001

★ ★ ★ ★

Apparently the Rufus Stone, in the New Forest in England, marks the spot where a bloke called Sir Walter Tyrrell, claimed as a forebear by these Tyrrells, shot King William II with an arrow. The Tyrrells might be drawing a long bow (boom-boom) but I have read, and indeed written, much sillier things on back labels. And this wine is as smooth as an arrow's trajectory with sweet berry fruit and vanilla from some light oak.

$24–26 Ⓕ

Tyrrell's Long Flat Red Cabernet Shiraz Malbec 2001

★ ★ ★ ☆

The Long Flat brand no longer belongs to Tyrrell's; it's now part of the burgeoning Cheviot Bridge Wine Company. Time will tell what this means, but given the record of the people behind Cheviot Bridge I'd reckon the Long Flat might become even better than this tasty little medium-bodied beauty. The Tyrrell's name has come off the label and snuck up onto the capsule, and soon it will just be plain old Long Flat, which is what we all called it anyhow.

$8–10 Ⓜ

Voyager Estate Shiraz 2001

★ ★ ★ ★

Not everyone will like this style but it deserves its place just because it is prepared to be different. On the nose and palate there are all sorts of wild and savoury notes along with pepper and spice—things you don't see too often in Aussie reds—that make it reminiscent of a Rhône Valley style from France. But the best thing is the lovely core of sweet fruit that supports all these savoury flavours and makes me think that in a few years this could be really very beautiful indeed.

$28–30 Ⓕ

Warburn Cabernet Merlot 2001

★ ★ ★ ★ ☆

Warburn is a winery on the move. Yet another Riverina producer which has started to make up ground on the better-established producers, the Warburn range of wines has no weaknesses. This cabernet merlot is clean as a whistle, with excellent structure and flavours—top stuff. They also make very good shiraz and semillon, so keep an eye out for the Warburn wines. (And let's face it, with that label they're hard to miss.)

$16–18 Ⓜ

Water Wheel Memsie Shiraz Malbec Cabernet Sauvignon 2001

★ ★ ★ ★

The Water Wheel winery at Bendigo has been creating some of the country's best-value rustic shiraz and cabernet sauvignon for close to thirty years. Memsie is the winery's first attempt that I can remember (bearing in mind I am very young and my memory is very bad) at making a softer, more everyday-drinking red wine. And it is a triumph. The fruit in this wine is crystal clear and the screwcap means it will cellar better for longer.

$16–18 Ⓕ 🍷

Western Range Cabernet Malbec 2002

★ ★ ★ ☆

This range of wines might possibly have the ugliest labels in Australia. Now I feel bad, so I'd best remind you that it is the stuff inside that counts and the Western Range wines, from vineyards around the Perth Hills, are terrific. I particularly like this wine with its 35% malbec, an underrated (including by me—see Winespeak) grape variety that adds colour and acid to the blend. I'd cellar this for a year or so and then it will really surprise and delight. Just make sure you serve it blind.

$14–16 Ⓜ

Wirra Wirra Church Block 2001

★ ★ ★ ★ ☆

Another wine that was experimentally bottled under screwcap this year, although the vast majority was still under cork. Church Block has been a staple on the table and in the cellar of wine lovers across Australia for donkeys' years and has always steered clear of overripe fruit and over-oaking. The 2001 is true to type with some excellent fruit definition, some savoury notes and good solid structure. A modest classic.

$20–22 Ⓕ 🍷

Wolf Blass Cabernet Merlot 2001

★ ★ ★ ☆

Given that all Wolf Blass labels have a defining colour, what would you call this—teal, perhaps? Wolf Blass Teal Label doesn't have much of a ring to it I'm afraid, but it seems a shame to let Port Adelaide corner the market in a whole colour…At any rate teal can only improve its own image by adorning this true-to-type Blass red. It is medium bodied and silky smooth with not a rough edge in sight, it tastes of berries and plums and it has 'drink me now' stamped all over it.

$14–16 Ⓜ

Wolf Blass Cabernet Sauvignon Yellow Label 2001

★ ★ ★ ★

When I was about nineteen, working in Surry Hills as a copy boy on a newspaper, there was a pub across the road that did a great steak. One lunchtime an extremely sophisticated young lady took me to lunch and bought a bottle of Wolf Blass Yellow Label. And I loved it, and so I began to drink more and, well, here I am today, some six or so years later, writing books about wine. And Yellow Label has lost none of its polish either—it's nice to know it's still such a good bet.

$14–16 Ⓜ

Wynns Coonawarra Cabernet Shiraz Merlot 2000

★ ★ ★ ★ ★

When I tasted this wine alongside many of its competitors, its class really shone through and so did the fact it was a year or two older than most others. This means it might be a little hard to find, but as we went to print I was assured it remained the current release on the shelves. I wouldn't worry though, because the 2001 will probably be just as good—rich, plummy, quite silky and with a very evident oak character on the nose and palate that marks it out from the crowd.

$16–18 Ⓕ

Wynns Coonawarra Cabernet Sauvignon 2000

★ ★ ★ ★ ☆

There will be no John Riddoch cabernet sauvignon from vintage 2000, so the fruit that would have gone into Wynns' premium cabernet has gone into this. Good news—at $50–60, the John Riddoch was always a bit of a stretch. Wynns Black Label is one of our classic wines and I have seen it on promotion for around $20. For that price it is an absolute steal: a beautiful cabernet sauvignon with lots of blackcurrant flavours and some fine tannins. And it will cellar.

$24–26 Ⓕ

Xanadu Secession Shiraz Cabernet Sauvignon 2002

★ ★ ★ ★

In my youth I was so in love with Olivia Newton John that I queued up and saw *Xanadu* on its first day of release. I don't care what you think, it's a fabulous movie and Andy Gibb was a great actor. And 'Wired for Sound' is a classic, which doesn't have anything to do with *Xanadu* apart from the roller skating in the film clip, but remains a fact. But about the wine: this is a well-balanced, medium-bodied wine that combines two great Australian varieties in elegant harmony—like Andy and ONJ.

$17–19 Ⓜ

Yalumba Merlot 2002

★ ★ ★ ★ ★   [best value red wine]

Merlot, as you may have gathered, is not my favourite grape variety in the same sense that Collingwood is not my favourite football team. Merlot is too often thin, over-hyped and over-priced and what annoys me most is this: if you can get a lovely tasty little number like the 'Y' for ten bucks (and I've seen it on special for under eight), why can't you get a *great* merlot when you fork out $30 or more? If you want merlot, buy $10 merlot. This is simple, juicy and quite delicious. Top stuff.

$9–11 Ⓜ

Yering Station ED Pinot Noir Rosé 2002

★ ★ ★ ★

The ED on the label stands for Extra Dry, which is a strong differentiating factor between this rosé and most others. This wine is certainly dry, and also a very pale pink colour, through a whisper of skin contact with the pinot noir juice. The result is quite delicious but if you want my opinion (you're going to get it anyway) this wine would be better with that little bit of extra sweetness. But then I guess they couldn't call it Extra Dry. If you want a 'serious' pink wine, then this is the one for you.

$17–19 Ⓛ

Zilzie Merlot 2002

★ ★ ★ ★

I don't know about you but I'm getting bored with the Zilzies. I mean their name isn't even Zilzie, it's Forbes, and their wines are so consistent you might be tempted to call them boring. But they're not boring, far from it; these wines are the future. They are cleverly made, well packaged and competitively priced—hell, I even like the merlot. We're going to be seeing, hearing and tasting a lot more Zilzies over the next few years so we'd all better get used to them.

$13–15 Ⓜ

Zilzie Shiraz 2002

★ ★ ★ ★ ★

A big, rich, plump, sweet and soft red wine that just needs a cosy night at home with a lover and a pizza. I can't organise the lover but the pizza's in the phone book (so to speak) and if you pop up to the Zilzie winery with both, maybe around the middle of the afternoon, I'm sure there will be somebody there to give you a bottle of the wine. Of course, now you're in Mildura you'll want to ditch that cold pizza and go to Stefano De Pieri's Grand Hotel for dinner—they serve the Zilzie shiraz anyway.

$13–15 Ⓕ

stickies & fortifieds

These proudly Australian wines are among the world's best but the sad fact is that fewer people than ever are drinking them. So dire is the situation that the Seppelt brand has taken the extraordinary step of repackaging all its sherries and fortified wines from 375 mL bottles into 750 mL bottles and *not increased the price*. Have you ever heard of anything like that? All the wines on the following pages are first rate, and there could be a whole lot more listed that are just as great. Try to find an opportunity to taste these wines some time soon—I promise they won't let you down.

All Saints Classic Muscat

★ ★ ★ ★

All Saints has become an important showpiece for the Rutherglen region. As you would expect they make some of the most delicious fortified wines in the area with nothing more than a split hair between this wine and the Classic Tokay at the same price. This muscat has floral aromatic notes that suggest some young components but it has the depth and richness on the palate to indicate that it also has plenty of the grand old stuff we love. A bargain at a touch over $20.

$22–25 500 mL

Baileys Founder Tokay

★ ★ ★ ★ ★

This wine blew me and a few judges away at the Adelaide Wine Show in 2002 when it collected the trophy for best fortified. We could hardly believe it was little old Baileys of Glenrowan. Even the chief winemaker of Beringer Blass, which owns Baileys, couldn't believe his eyes when the wine's identity was revealed. This is wonderful tokay with aromas of tea leaf and that wonderfully complex palate and luscious sweetness that make you want to keep drinking it forever.

$18–20 750 mL

Brown Brothers Reserve Muscat

★ ★ ★ ★ ★

I'm still a bit confused about this wine. It just seems to have too much intensity and richness for a wine at this price. It makes me think the winemakers at Brown Brothers have done the old switcheroo with a much more expensive and older product to convince people to drink more fortified wine. Well, we all would if more of them tasted like this—all nuts and raisins and Christmas pudding-like. An incredible wine at the price.

$18–20 750 mL

De Bortoli Noble One 2000

★ ★ ★ ★ ☆

There are now more competitors than ever for the mantle of Australia's best sticky, but you have to judge these things over time and therefore the trophy still belongs here. The Noble One was the first wine that showed we could do something really special with botrytis-infected semillon in this country, and it continues to impress. Recent vintages have been a little lighter and that's good—it means that finishing a bottle isn't so much of a challenge.

$20–22 375 mL

McWilliam's Riverina Botrytis Semillon 2000

★ ★ ★ ★

This may be the wine that is pushing hardest against the De Bortoli Noble One for the title of best sticky in the country. Certainly the wine show judges like this wine, as every vintage seems to have at least half a dozen gold medals on its chest. This is a more alcoholic wine than the Noble One, suggesting the grapes were a little riper when they were picked. The palate is unctuous, very intensely marmalade-like, but still fresh on the finish. Wonderful sweet wine.

$20–22 375 mL

Miranda Golden Botrytis 2001

★ ★ ★ ★ ★

This has been one of the best dessert wines in Australia for some time and the current vintage seems destined to carry on a proud tradition. Made from botrytis-affected grapes from the Miranda vineyards in the Riverina, this is a terrific wine to finish any meal. It has lovely aromas and flavours of marmalade and honey with a wonderfully well-balanced palate. It just makes me want to get into a big bowl of fruit salad and finish the bottle.

$17–19 375 mL

Morris Liqueur Tokay
★ ★ ★ ★

The fortified wines of Morris—where exactly should I start? Quite honestly, this wine and the muscat for the same price are no better or worse in terms of quality than they were ten years ago. So does that mean we should ignore them and find something new? Not when the old is as good and consistent as this. Think of this as your favourite Italian restaurant—you might try the flash new trendy ones but which one do you want to go back to time after time?

$16–18 500 mL

Penfolds Club Tawny
★ ★ ★ ★

Club Port has some sexy new packaging to snap it into line with the rest of the Penfolds wines and it has never looked better. The quality of the port which we're no longer allowed to call port isn't too bad either. The wine has lovely caramel and toffee characters and some nuttiness, but the finish manages still to be fresh which is important in fortified wine. When this is on special below $10 it's a bargain.

$10–12 750 mL

RL Buller Fine Old Tawny

★ ★ ★ ★

The Bullers have two wineries, one at Swan Hill and this one at Rutherglen that has access to some of the greatest fortified material in the region. This is indeed a fine old tawny with a lovely rusty colour, some nutty almondy notes and a sweet palate that makes you think of caramel and honey snaps. This is the wine to bring out when someone turns up to dinner with one of those stinky blue cheeses. Mmmmm…blue cheese and port. Yum.

$20–22 750 mL

Seppelt Show Amontillado DP 116

★ ★ ★ ★ ☆

As with the entire Seppelt range, the packaging of this wine has changed again so if you can't find it on the shelf, chances are you're looking straight at it. This beautiful nutty, slightly off-dry sherry is a terrific aperitif but equally a top wine with a soup, particularly beef consommé with mushrooms for some reason. And by the way, we can't call it sherry any more because that word is owned by the Spanish. This is one of the new great-value 750 mL bottles.

$20–24 750 mL

Seppelt Tokay DP 37

★ ★ ★ ★ ★ [best value sweet win

Please don't ask me to explain the DP 37 bit or for that matter the myriad different fortified wines in the new Seppelt range (actually the old Seppelt range in new outfits). Just drink it and ask no questions. This is an unctuous, sweet, toffee-like wine that is almost embarrassingly good at the price. It has some older material to give it complexity, just a hint of nuttiness and enough acid so it doesn't taste sickly sweet. A classic tokay at an unbeatable price—even more unbeatable since they doubled the size of the bottle.

$18–20 750 mL

something special

sparklings
& champagne

Australia makes some terrific sparklers even though as a rule they're not really my thing. But as for French bubbles— well to be honest you can give me as much as you like as often as you like. Like everyone I have my favourites, which are based as much on brand recognition as flavour, but in my world any French is good French. I hope that doesn't sound smutty.

Bollinger Special Cuvée NV

Still my favourite and no matter how many times people try to tell me this or that champagne is better than Bolly, I stick to my guns. You see drinking champagne is about more than just drinking, it's about the message you are sending to those with whom you choose to share. Louis Roederer and Billecart Salmon are for wine snobs, Moët is for poseurs, Veuve Clicquot is for wannabes and Bollinger is for fair dinkum people who just want to get on with it and have fun.

$65–75

Piper Heidsieck NV

Piper is certainly the best value French bubbles if you have the occasion but not quite the budget. You should be able to find it on special for less than $50 and at that price it's damn good value. In the old days Piper's quality used to match its low price, but not any more. The wine is as good as those from most of the better-known Champagne houses and in fact it surpasses one or two extremely well-known brands that might be $20 a bottle more expensive. Seek it out.

$45–55

Stefano Lubiana NV Brut

A couple of years back poor Steve Lubiana got in terrible strife when Veuve Clicquot ordered him to change the colour of his label, which they thought was too close to their famous orange one. The fact they took a poor little Tasmanian like Steve to court really upset me and I have refused to drink Veuve since (although in fact no one has yet given me a chance to test my resolve). Try this top Tassie sparkler instead—it's fresh and delicious and *so* not orange.

$30–35

Taittinger NV

Remember the image thing? (See Bollinger.) Taittinger is an understated brand that demonstrates your class. Despite my devotion to another brand (see Bollinger), this is the wine I would drink if I wanted people to think I was a bit mysterious. You don't see it much, so you might not know whether it's desperately expensive, and it is a subtle, wonderfully finessed wine that doesn't leap out at you and slap you about the face. I think Catherine Deneuve would enjoy Taittinger.

$60–70

Yarrabank Cuvée 1999

I think this is probably the best Australian sparkling wine being made at the moment. From the winemakers at Champagne Devaux in France, this wine is made at the wonderful Yering Station complex in the Yarra Valley. It tastes and smells quite a bit like 'real' champagne, meaning that the wine boasts a bit of yeast-derived complexity and some nuttiness and creaminess on the palate. The wine has lovely acidity and the finish is quite long and fine—this is terrific stuff.

$34–36

upmarket whites

With all the fuss made about the quality of Australian red wines it is sometimes forgotten that we also make some of the best white wines in the world. Whites of complexity and great beauty, whites made from riesling, chardonnay and semillon in particular. So go on, spoil yourself once in a while. Pick up a special bottle and see what difference a few extra bucks can make.

Bindi Chardonnay 2001

Can I name drop? Well, we were having dinner with Rick Stein, the fish guy from the TV, and my wife ordered a glass of Bindi chardonnay. Rick and I both had a taste and before you could say 'Hey, is that Aristos on the next table?' (it was) we had finished three bottles of the stuff. Rick thinks it goes incredibly well with kingfish but we bumped into Jamie Oliver later, and he thought char-grilled scallops. This is right up there with my favourite chardies of the year. 03 5428 2564.

$34–36

Brokenwood ILR Semillon 1997

Marvellously toasty with a hint of honey, this is what aged Hunter semillon is all about. If I consumed nothing but this wine and the Tyrrell's Vat 1 for the next six months, I'd be quite happy—although perhaps a little peckish. 'ILR' is the winemaker and MD of Brokenwood, Iain Leslie Riggs (or Insular Lazy Recalcitrant, as one of his staff suggested). Riggs is a terrific winemaker and Brokenwood is one of the most reliable brands on the market. The 1998 will be out soon and it is just as good.

$34–36

Grosset Piccadilly Chardonnay 2002

Jeff Grosset is the man who stood tall and said that riesling was getting a bum steer, and by making his Polish Hill and Watervale rieslings he set the tone for the long-awaited (is it here yet?) riesling revival. And then of course there are screwcaps. From vintage 2003 Jeff will bottle more than ninety per cent of his wines, both red and white, under screwcap; undoubtedly a man of vision. This is one of the ten best chardonnays in the country—delicious, focussed, beautifully balanced and powerful. Quite a triumph.

$45–48

Lake's Folly Chardonnay 2001

If you are really old you will remember Lake's Folly fondly. It was one of the first boutique wineries in Australia, set up in the Hunter Valley in 1963 by Dr Max Lake, blazing the trail for the multitude of doctors and lawyers who have started their own winemaking follies since then. Lake's Folly still produces one of the best Hunter chardonnays. It combines elegance and complexity and makes a strong case for the Hunter as a genuine premium chardonnay region.

$36–40

Lenton Brae Chardonnay 2001

I've been keeping an eye on Lenton Brae as they slowly climbed the ladder of Margaret River producers. This wine may not have the reputation of a Cullen, Leeuwin or Cape Mentelle just yet but if they keep making them like this, it won't be long. I tasted this wine with a group of winemakers and some of the best and most expensive chardonnays in the country and it came out tops. Wonderfully made, complex, nutty, long and delicious—seek it out.

$28–30

Mitchelton Airstrip Marsanne Roussanne Viognier 2002

This was a favourite of mine last year and I still love the 2001 enough to suggest that if you can find it you should pick some up. I'm not usually one to be following fashion, but I do like the trend for blending these three exotic varieties together like they do in France's Rhône Valley. The result is a soft, well-balanced wine with some honeysuckle and citrus characters and a really interesting palate—proof that variety is indeed the spice of life.

$26–30

Petaluma Chardonnay 2001

Brian Croser's Petaluma brand is one you have to love if you're going to exhibit any semblance of cool among winelovers. You have to understand the focussed restraint and the almost waif-like elegance. This is Armani winemaking. At first, you see what isn't there—no frills—and it looks a bit basic. But the longer you look and the more other garish rubbish you see, the more you appreciate the art of restraint and the power of leaving things out. This is an intellectual wine and to be honest I'm probably too stupid for it.

$38–40

Pooles Rock Chardonnay 2001

A few years back this wine was absolutely the grooviest white wine in the grooviest restaurants in Sydney. Admittedly I don't travel to the groovy places in Sydney that often, but I get the impression this wine might not be as white hot now. I have no idea why, because it's still one of the best Hunter chardonnays, with lovely creamy and toasty characters, and it's picked up medals and trophies around the place. How much groovier do you want?

$25–27

Scorpo Pinot Gris 2002

The Scorpo wines were more fashionable than hair braids in 2003 and this little pinot gris, matured in old oak barrels at Scorpo-world on Victoria's Mornington Peninsula, is quite delicious. When I say 'little', however, please take it with a grain of salt. The wine comes in at a pretty healthy 14% alcohol (so don't plan to drive home after a few glasses) but the high alcohol is necessary to give the wine its lovely pear-like varietal characters.

$26–28

Seppelt Jaluka Chardonnay 2000

The Jaluka back label says it's sourced from the famous Seppelt Drumborg vineyard near Portland in south-west Victoria. So is it the old Drumborg chardonnay with a new name? Yes and no, say the makers inscrutably. Whatever that might mean, I frankly don't care if this wine calls itself Victoria Beckham—when I tasted it I was blown away by its sheer beauty. It has length, complexity and absolute, unadulterated deliciousness and it's one of the best chardonnays in the country.

$28–30

Shaw and Smith M3 Chardonnay 2001

Shaw and Smith are best known for their fresh, racy sauvignon blanc but they can turn their hand to chardonnay too, it seems. This wine has had the Rolls Royce treatment right down the line, so it's a good one to taste if you want the experience of dead posh chardonnay without doing $70 or more for the likes of Giaconda or Cullen. Lovely creamy flavours, a fine, beautifully balanced palate and terrific acidity combine to make it one of the few Australian chardonnays you might cellar.

$32–36

Stonier Reserve Chardonnay 2001

The Stonier Reserve wines are close to the best combination of quality and value on the Mornington Peninsula. Yes, $38 is a fair whack, but this wine would give a few $100+ French burgundies a run for their money, so it's all relative. Anyway, you need to know what to drink when the boss buys you dinner and tells you money is no object (no, it's never happened to me either; but then I work for myself). The 2000 was voted best chardonnay in the world in London; this is a little richer, with nuances of honeysuckle and wonderful mouthfeel.

$36–40

Torbreck Viognier Marsanne Roussanne 2002

It's not very often I can claim to have planted the vines that have provided the fruit for a top wine, which is probably because I have only ever planted one vineyard. It was Torbreck's Barossa Valley viognier vineyard, where for a full weekend back in 1994 we broke our backs sticking little cuttings into the ground. And what did we get for our hardship? Well, the satisfaction that at least the winemaker hasn't gone and stuffed up all our hard work. This is delicious and very rich. Drink with full flavoured roast chook and vegies.

$34–36

Tyrrell's Vat 1 Semillon 1997

I know I carry on about this wine every year, but I'm going to persist until everyone agrees it is the best white wine in Australia. The 1997 is not quite as good as the 1996—but that's like saying pashing Elle Macpherson doesn't quite measure up to snogging Cameron Diaz. This soft, low alcohol, toasty beauty has only one shortcoming and that is the silly bit of bark stuck in the neck of the bottle. Of all the wines available, aged Hunter semillon needs the screwcap most.

$45–50

superior reds

Go on, you know you want to. You want to know what all the fuss is about with these expensive wines, you want to find out if a wine that costs $50 is that much better than the ones you normally drink for $10. Well here's your chance. Check these out and make up your own mind whether the posh wines I like to drink on special occasions are better than the ones you like to drink most of the time.

Ata Rangi Pinot Noir 2001 NZ

This wine comes from Wairapara on New Zealand's North Island and is the best pinot noir made south of the equator. There you go, who said wine writers were all wishy-washy and scared to make definitive statements? It has a stunningly exotic, perfumed nose and a supple, silky, delicious palate with flavours that seem to linger forever. This is for anyone who ever wondered why people get worked up about pinot noir: it's because when we taste a wine like this we go to Nirvana. No it doesn't smell like teen spirit.

$65–70

Balnaves Coonawarra Cabernet Sauvignon 2000

Ask the average wine drinker to name their top Coonawarra names and you will probably not find Balnaves on the list. Why? Because they're small, they sell most of their wine direct from the winery and they go about their excellent business without fuss. Pete Bissell is the form winemaker of the region and looking likely to keep going that way; and this wine is a wonderful expression of Coonawarra—rich cassis flavours, lovely fine tannins, and damn good value. 08 8737 2946.

$30–32

Cape Mentelle Shiraz 2001

This wine has lovely earthy, leathery, savoury characters and very much reminds me of a more European style of wine. That's the wonderful thing about the Margaret River wines— they are beginning to define their own style, very much out of the mainstream of Australian blockbuster shiraz. And Cape Mentelle is just *so* fashionable. If you are having a dinner party with friends who wear black skivvies and dark-rimmed glasses, this is the wine for them. They won't just be impressed—they'll think you're an architect.

$30–32

Clonakilla Shiraz Viognier 2002

The 2001 was one of the best Australian reds of the past ten years and the '02 is not far behind. Magnificent aromatics courtesy of ripe, spicy shiraz and a twist of exotic viognier, and a long, fine, beautifully structured palate that sings a love song to your tongue. If you like red wine with real character and quality, I strongly suggest that you get yourself on the mailing list. The shiraz viognier sells out incredibly quickly each year so don't be tardy. 02 6227 5877.

$48–50

Cullen Diana Madeline Cabernet Merlot 2001

Still the best cabernet sauvignon-based wine in Australia, with one change this year: the label. Vanya Cullen has finally done what she has long wanted to do and named the flagship wine after her wonderful mother Di, who passed away early in 2003. Di Cullen was a pioneer of Margaret River and one of the greats of Australian wine history—and the fact that she has this wonderful wine named after her is a fine and fitting legacy. Beautifully structured wine that needs eight years to be at its best.

$70–75

Curlewis Pinot Noir 2001

Curlewis is my find of the year. When I first ran into winery owner Rainer Breit I thought he was quite a character; then I tasted his wines and now I like him even more. The winery is on the Bellarine Peninsula near Geelong, and the pinots from 2000 and 2001 are both stunning. They also make a very good spicy shiraz. You'll have to call Rainer (03 5250 4567) to buy some wine— just remember to tell him Stuart sent you. You never know, he might send me something for free.

$36–40

Mountadam Shiraz 2001

This Eden Valley outfit knows its own worth and frankly their wines have never grabbed me as being super value. But this new shiraz is very good, and certainly worth serious consideration if you're in the market for something special. The wine has lovely rich fruit, a hint of cool-climate spice and a beautifully structured palate. Would say yes (actually it would probably say *oui* as the winery has just been bought by the French) to boeuf bourguignon.

$40–44

Mount Langi Ghiran Shiraz 2000

Mount Langi, at the foot of the Grampians, produces one of the great shiraz wines of Australia. Over the years it's stuck to its guns and survived the slings and arrows of outrageous trends, and come out of it better than ever. The classic calling card of this Western Victorian shiraz is the pepper and spice character on the nose that follows through onto the palate without ever overshadowing the core of beautiful fruit. We've also had a sneak preview of the 2001 and we love it.

$48–50

Palliser Estate Pinot Noir 2001 NZ

One of New Zealand's most consistent pinots and likely to be more widely available than the hedonistic and elusive Ata Rangi. But there's no need to compare this wine with anything—just enjoy its aromatic bouquet, its soft and complex palate and the seductively smooth tannins that would make it taste like silk if silk tasted like anything. This wine is better than around 99 per cent of Australian pinots and, for pinot noir, it's not terribly expensive. Definitely one for the posh dinner party.

$36–40

Penfolds Grange 1998

Has there ever been a bigger fuss than the fuss that surrounded the launch of the 1998 Grange? Not in my lifetime. So—what does this $400 bottle of Aussie wine taste like? Is it worth the hoo-hah? Is it indeed the greatest wine ever made in Australia? The answers are: very nice, probably not and we don't think so (a show of hands in the *Don't Buy Wine Without Me* office nominated Lindemans Bin 65 Chardonnay). Certainly the 1998 Grange is a wonderful wine, imperious and loaded with everything from oak to ultra-ripe fruit but when the question of value arises I get all confused. You see drinking a bottle of Grange feels *different* and that is the key. Yes, it *is* just a bottle of wine (as we always say sniffily when an old one goes at auction for a four-figure sum) and yes, $400 *is* a ridiculous price; but it is Grange and drinking Grange isn't like drinking anything else we produce in this country. Try it once for yourself; and try not to touch it until at least ten years after vintage.

$350–400

Plantagenet Shiraz 2001

The southern parts of Western Australia are becoming home to great shiraz—lovely, spicy shiraz that has more in common with those from the cooler climes of Victoria than the warmer regions of South Australia. I've thought for a long time that the Plantagenet shiraz was just about the best shiraz to come out of WA and the 2001 gives me no reason to recant. A richly intense wine with a typical spicy character and lovely nuance of black cherries, it drinks beautifully at five to eight years of age.

$40–44

Rochford Macedon Ranges Pinot Noir 2001

Now repeat after me…Rochford not Rockford. Having done some work over the years for both wineries I always find it amusing when people seek out big rich shiraz from Rochford and fine elegant pinot noir from Rockford. The two wineries couldn't be any more different, with Rochford tucked into the cool hills around Macedon where they make fine pinot and Rockford being the home of rustic shiraz in the Barossa. This one's the gorgeous smooth pinot, OK?

$38–40

{superior reds} 145

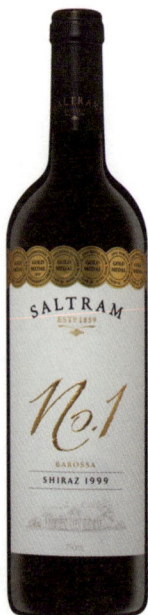

Saltram No.1 Barossa Shiraz 1999

If someone asked me why I love Barossa shiraz so much I would show them two wines: this Saltram and the Rockford Basket Press shiraz. Quite different styles, but they both show the Barossa at its best. This wine is more readily available than the Rockford, however, so it gets the gig. It's densely packed with rich, juicy, sweet fruit and plenty of supporting oak that doesn't seem to intrude but to complement. It may sound like a monster, but in fact it's a sophisticated, well-balanced wine. Marvellous stuff.

$60–65

Scorpo Shiraz 2001

Every wine writer in the country has an opinion on this wine, ranging through every shade of criticism— from one of the greatest shirazes ever tasted through to stinky, poopy and not very nice at all. I work every day of my life in the presence of a Scorpo so guess what I reckon: it's tops. But moral cowardice aside, I like this wine because it's out of the mainstream, with spicy, savoury flavours like very few others in this country—and it proves shiraz can grow on the Mornington Peninsula.

$30–32

Seppelt St Peters Shiraz 1999

Seppelt is on the move, and you will have noticed a couple of their new 'Victorian' range wines among my best-value picks. Well, if you want to go the hog and drink something really special, tuck into this gem. It's from the St Peters vineyard in Great Western and it is truly beautiful Victorian shiraz, with suppleness, intensity, flavours of dark berries and smoky oak and beautiful tannin. Seppelt is part of Southcorp, which also produces Grange; and I'd say this would have to be the company's second-best shiraz.

$48–52

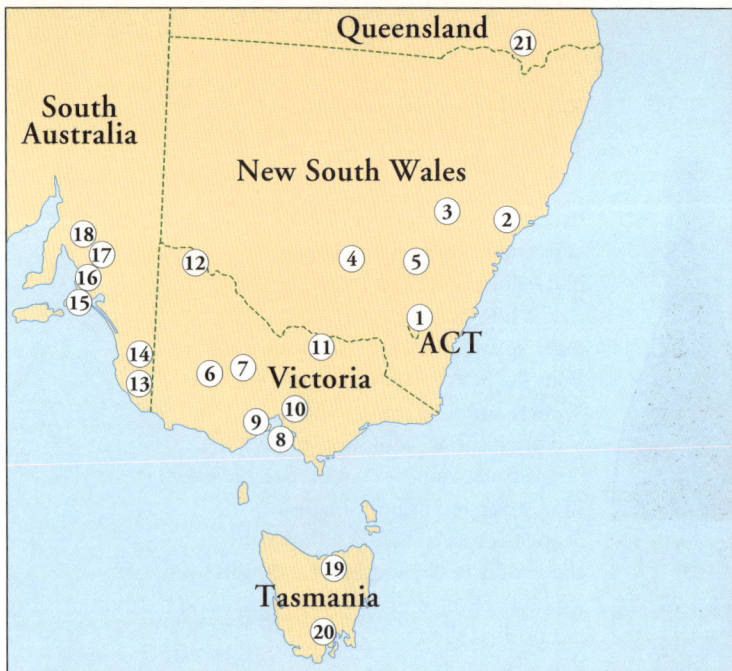

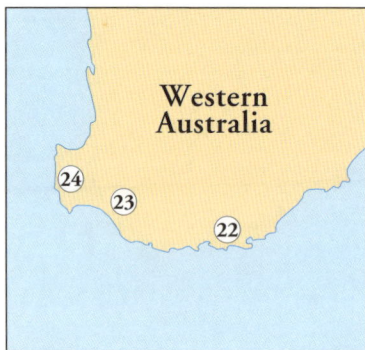

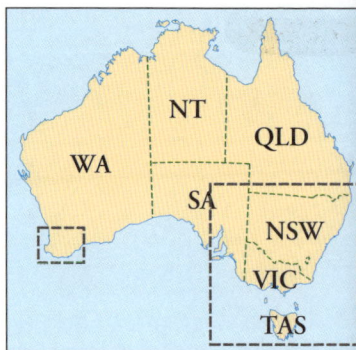

① Canberra Region	⑨ Bellarine Peninsula/Geelong	⑯ Adelaide Hills
② Hunter Valley	⑩ Yarra Valley	⑰ Barossa Valley
③ Mudgee	⑪ North-east Victoria	⑱ Clare Valley
④ Riverina/Griffith	⑫ North-west Victoria	⑲ Tamar Valley
⑤ Central NSW	⑬ Coonawarra	⑳ Huon Valley
⑥ Great Western/Grampians	⑭ Padthaway	㉑ Granite Belt
⑦ Pyrenees	⑮ McLaren Vale	㉒ Great Southern
⑧ Mornington Peninsula		㉓ Pemberton/Manjimup
		㉔ Margaret River

regions

Sitting at home and drinking wine is all well and good, but you should probably get out more. And what better holiday plan could you have than cruising around this beautiful country, seeing the sights, exploring your heritage and drinking wine? Of course there is plenty of Australia where you can be several hours away from the nearest wine-producing region even by fast jet; but most of us don't live there. If you are in any of the capital cities except Darwin— even Brisbane—there is a flourishing wine centre only a couple of hours away. So this is more or less a touring guide to each of the major wine-producing regions in Australia. In it you will find a brief outline of what makes each region unique, what you should look out for and where you will taste the best wines.

But first, a word from our sponsors, the Australian wine industry, who wish you to stay alive long enough to consume plenty more of their product:

Be careful about drinking and driving.

Those abstemious little sips you consider so thoughtfully at the wineries can add up surprisingly fast. Under no circumstances should you try to drive back to the city after a day's tasting. Wine regions are absolutely carpeted with great little B&Bs and other accommodation—why not make a real weekend of it? If you can't do that, my advice is to appoint a designated driver who can pace himself or herself, or take it in turns for each day of tasting so no one misses out.

ACT / Canberra

Still up and coming and fighting a valiant battle against the high-country cold, the Canberra region, most of which is actually in NSW, can produce excellent chardonnay, pinot noir and riesling. BRL Hardy recently opened their Kamberra wine tourism centre at Lyneham, just one of the signs that the area is starting to be taken seriously by the big producers. Most of the vineyards in the region survived the fires of January 2003 although the hot and dry conditions are likely to have an impact on final wine quality; certainly quantity will be reduced.

Best varieties riesling, chardonnay, pinot noir, viognier.

Best recent vintages 1997, 1998, 2001, 2002.

Best producers Clonakilla, Lark Hill, Brindabella Hills, Helm Wines.

Best bet While undoubtedly the Clonakilla Shiraz Viognier is the star wine of the Canberra district you would be well served to have a good look at all of the wines from the Lark Hill winery, over near Lake George. The winery is at Bungendore at an altitude of almost 900m making it one of the highest vineyard sites in the country. There is not a dud wine in the Lark Hill range with the pinot noir, riesling and chardonnay all seriously excellent wines—the pinot noir is certainly my favourite from this region.

New South Wales
Hunter Valley

It's Sydney's playground, the Hunter Valley, so not surprisingly it's the most visited wine region in Australia and is being developed faster than a set of holiday snaps. The wines are moving with the times, too. Aged semillon has always been the Hunter's peerless product but it's a mite austere for some, as are the classic pungent, savoury reds from this area. The producers are starting to turn their hands to some more accessible, crowd-pleasing styles and having a fair crack at—guess what—chardonnay.

Best varieties semillon, shiraz, verdelho and chardonnay.

Best recent vintages 1995, 1998, 2000.

Best producers Tyrrells, Brokenwood, McWilliam's, Margan, Capercaillie.

Best bet If you like old semillon, a day or two in the Hunter is like being in heaven. At Tyrrells alone you could hang around all afternoon although they tend to kick me out around 3 p.m. when I start back on the first wines I had in the morning. If you like your whites a bit sweeter, try the verdelhos and don't ignore the oft-overlooked virtues of Hunter chardonnay. If Lake's Folly is open you must visit and taste their cabernet and chardonnay—two classics. Apart from Lake's Folly, stick with shiraz, which is clearly the best red variety in the region, and steer clear of pinot noir and riesling—they simply shouldn't be planted here.

Mudgee

It's tosh to talk about Mudgee as a 'new region'—
they were growing grapes there in 1858—but it's
certainly come into its own in the last few years.
There are some truly excellent red wines coming out
of Mudgee, and not only shiraz and cabernet
sauvignon—the newer Italian varieties like
sangiovese and barbera are coming up too.

Best varieties chardonnay, sangiovese, shiraz,
cabernet sauvignon.

Best recent vintages 1996, 1998, 2001, 2002.

Best producers Montrose, Andrew Harris,
Huntington Estate and Rosemount Estate.

Best bet Mudgee can always surprise you. Just
when it's got you thinking it's a red wine region
you stumble upon a really lovely chardonnay and
you have to think again. The best wines, however,
are the more robust style reds—the Rosemount
Mountain Blue red wine is certainly the best ever
to come from Mudgee and their Hill of Gold wines
are terrific as well. By the way, if you want to make
a weekend of it in Mudgee, go the weekend of the
Mudgee picnic races—awesome fun.

Riverina / Griffith / Murrumbidgee
Irrigation Area

We haven't seen the last of that sensational Riverina
2002 vintage yet—if you keep looking you should
still be able to get hold of some great red and white
bargains through to the end of 2004. The other
celebrity product of the region is of course the
perennially superlative dessert wine, which goes
like a train here because of the hospitable
environment the area's climate creates for *Botrytis
cinerea*, the noble rot.

It's an odd one really—on the one hand this area produces the best dessert wines in Australia, some of which would be quite comfortable on the world stage. On the other, it houses a monster industrial setup responsible for 15% of the country's bulk grape production, much of which goes into budget wines and casks. Go figure.

Best varieties botrytised wines, sauvignon blanc, white blends, shiraz.

Best recent vintages 1997, 1998, 2000, 2002.

Best producers McWilliam's Hanwood, West End, Miranda, Cookoothama and De Bortoli.

Best bet Around here you can get great wines for around $10 because it is cheap to grow grapes and the good irrigation system means growers can get plenty of grapes per hectare. For the past two years the West End winery has been making some amazing wines at ridiculously cheap prices. At Casella they do much the same. And at De Bortoli things are pretty similar…

Central NSW (Cowra, Orange, Hilltops)

Vineyards were first planted commercially round Orange in 1983 at Bloodwood Estate, so it's another area only recently starting to be developed. But it's graced by some of the best viticultural land in Australia—and some of the highest, at up to 1000 metres above sea level. This is traditionally orchard country but the number of vineyards is growing all the time. Cowra has been going a bit longer, and specialises in producing superior chardonnay for the big Hunter-based wineries. The area around Young, known as the Hilltops, is going places with its shiraz and cabernet sauvignon. It's currently best known, though, for McWilliam's

Barwang range, which offers top quality at a very fair price.

Best varieties Orange—chardonnay, merlot. Young—shiraz, cabernet sauvignon. Cowra—chardonnay.

Best recent vintages 1998, 2001, 2002.

Best producers Canobolas, Rosemount Orange, McWilliam's Barwang.

Best bet Because this is a relatively remote area without that many wineries there aren't that many cellar door options, so make sure you ring ahead to your favourite winery to see if they are open. Chances are if someone answers they will be happy to show you around and let you taste a few wines. Also if you visit Orange don't, whatever you do, miss out on having a meal at Selkirks—it is one of the best regional restaurants in NSW.

Victoria
Great Western / Grampians

This is great territory for red wine. Shiraz in particular grows rich and spicy and delicious in this area, and cabernet blends are also consistently good. Careful though—they often have a minty taste that people either love or loathe.

Best varieties shiraz, chardonnay, riesling.

Best recent vintages 1997, 1998, 2000, 2002, 2003.

Best producers Seppelt Great Western, Mount Langi Ghiran, Best's Great Western.

Best bet This really is good shiraz country but the style of wines is nothing like those of the Barossa or McLaren Vale in South Australia. Over here the wines are peppery, a little spicy and quite savoury rather than sweet in style. Its also a great area for sparkling shiraz and just about the best in the country come from Seppelt Great Western. If you visit Great Western Seppelt is a must, but also pop your head in at Best's—the Thompson family at Bests have been making some vastly under-rated wines in the region for more than a century. Their shiraz and rieslings are superb.

Pyrenees

The Central Victorian Pyrenees, you idiot, not the French–Spanish border area—we're talking about Avoca, Moonambel, Kara Kara and Redbank. The French do get a look in, however, because they kicked off the wine industry in this region at Chateau Remy in the mid-1960s (it's now called Blue Pyrenees). Reds predominate here, but the cooler southern end of the region produces some good sparkling wines.

Best varieties shiraz, merlot, chardonnay and pinot noir.

Best recent vintages 1997, 1998, 2000, 2002.

Best producers Dalwhinnie, Blue Pyrenees Estate, Taltarni, Redbank, Mount Avoca.

Best bet The Pyrenees may be Australia's pétanque centre. There are several competitions run each year near Avoca which might have something to do with the fact that two of the biggest wineries in the region—Blue Pyrenees and Taltarni—were both set up by French companies. Both of the aforementioned wineries also make great bubbles to celebrate your win on the *piste*.

Mornington Peninsula

Salt, sea air, proximity to the city—no wonder land on the Peninsula is expensive. Following a basic law of economics, the wines are too, by and large, so take your credit card. And another piece of advice—take the car with the GPS, this region is the most confusing and poorly signposted in Australia. You are almost guaranteed to get lost a couple of times in a day. The Mornington Peninsula is cool-climate, marginal country where vineyards abut championship golf courses and lifestyle is the overriding motivation for many of the small wineries dotted throughout the region. The wines are always fine, light to medium bodied and at their best in warm vintages although better viticultural practices are making it a more consistent place these days. Chardonnay and pinot noir—*definitely* pinot noir—are the two best grapes although there is a growing following for pinot grigio and, believe it or not, a couple of decent shirazes have appeared in recent years.

Best varieties pinot noir, pinot grigio, chardonnay.

Best recent vintages 1997, 1998, 2000, 2002.

Best producers Stonier, Paringa Estate, Ten Minutes by Tractor, Scorpo, Kooyong.

Best bet The standard of wines on the Mornington Peninsula is still improving as the traditional hobby winemakers are joined by the pros. 2000 and 2001 produced truly great pinots noirs and the chardonnays from 2002 and also possibly 2003 are outstanding too.

If you love golf the Peninsula is unquestionably the greatest wine and golf region in Australia.

There are not only more championship courses per square kilometer than just about anywhere in the world, the best public access course in the country, the Dunes, is nestled snugly there amongst a few good wineries.

Bellarine Peninsula / Geelong

The Geelong region was vital to the Victorian wine industry in the 1860s and 1870s but was the first to be affected by the vine louse phylloxera. All the vines in the region were pulled out in the 1880s in a vain attempt to halt the disease, which went on to devastate the industry throughout the colony. The region was replanted in the 1970s and the industry here is slowly gathering momentum. Pinot noir and chardonnay are the blue-ribbon varieties, particularly in warmer vintages, and shiraz is gaining a real following. This region is simply too cool for decent cabernet sauvignon in my opinion.

Best varieties pinot noir, chardonnay, shiraz.

Best recent vintages 1997, 2000, 2001, 2002.

Best producers Scotchman's Hill, Bannockburn, Curlewis.

Best bet The region's most famous winery, Bannockburn, doesn't have a cellar door, but you should definitely visit the Pettavel winery where, apart from a collection of good albeit fairly pricey wines, they have an extraordinarily good restaurant—as good as any at a winery in Australia. If they have any pigeon on the menu, try it—it is one of the best dishes in the country.

Yarra Valley

The Yarra Valley produces some of our very best pinot noir, great chardonnay and occasionally brilliant cabernet sauvignon and merlot; also some excellent dairy pasture. Produce and food, in fact, are growing in importance alongside grapes in the Yarra which makes the area—an hour from Melbourne—a pretty impressive foodie tourist mecca.

Best varieties sauvignon blanc, merlot, pinot noir, chardonnay.

Best recent vintages 1997, 1998, 2000, 2002.

Best producers Coldstream Hills, De Bortoli, Punt Road, Yering Station.

Best bet Lots of holiday facilities including the new Jack Nicklaus-designed golf course, outstanding accommodation and plenty of good cellar doors with restaurants. It is most definitely a two-day stay. If you are there for two days I would counsel lunch at De Bortoli one of those days, a visit to the Rochford winery for a concert, bubbles at Chandon and a few cold beers at the Healesville pub—and have a great day.

North-East Victoria

Welcome to Kelly country. This is where you get those powerhouse warm-climate reds—shiraz and durif—full enough of flavour and richness to make your grandfather weep with nostalgia. It's the fortified wines, however, that are truly exceptional here—any number of the Rutherglen and Milawa tokays or muscats could claim to be among the world's best sweet fortified wines. The 'newer' and sub-regions of the north-east are higher and cooler and they are making some of the most interesting styles in Australia. The Alpine and King valleys are home to many second-generation Italian–Australian families who are having a fling at grapes like sangiovese, barbera and nebbiolo and in addition to these Italian varieties there's also experimentation in other less known varieties—as far as I know this is the only region in Australia where you can taste saperavi, pinot grigio, petit manseng and chardonnay all at the same cellar door! Vintage 2003 was one of the toughest in living memory in these parts as fires ravaged much of Victoria's north east. Many grapes came to the wineries smelling of smoke and the character only got worse as the wines fermented. Much of this wine was 'fixed' by some new technology but some growers suffered when wineries didn't want to buy their fruit. Let's hope they have a great and bountiful 2004.

Best varieties shiraz, durif, riesling, sangiovese, tempranillo.

Best recent vintages 1996, 1998, 2000, 2002.

Best producers Morris, Chambers Rosewood, Stanton and Killeen, Brown Brothers, Gapsted, Pizzini.

Best bet In Rutherglen, stick with reds and fortifieds: you will never go wrong. If you are down in the King Valley around Milawa, though, it's time to go crazy and get stuck into the obscure grape varieties with origins all over Europe. The best place to start with all these weird grapes is at Brown Brothers, where there is also a terrific restaurant. After the wine pop down the road to the Milawa Cheese Factory and indulge in some of the best and most fattening cheeses in Australia.

North-West Victoria

Many of the vineyards up here on the banks of the mighty Murray are actually across the border in New South Wales, so we won't get too dogmatic about the state divisions. The main thing is that these irrigated areas produce high yields of fruit from relatively inexpensive land and that means: cheap wine (and I mean that in the nicest possible way). Like their cousins in the Riverina, the winemakers around the river drive the massive volumes of under-$10 bottled wines and our ever-popular 'bags in a box'. They also had their greatest vintage ever in 2002 and a pretty good one, although a bit hot and dry, in 2003.

Best varieties chardonnay, shiraz, merlot, viognier.

Best recent vintages 1998, 1999, 2001, 2002.

Best producers Trentham Estate, Mildara, Deakin Estate, Zilzie.

Best bet These days Sunraysia, and Mildura in particular, are most famously home to Stefano De Pieri and his restaurant and gondola. Stefano's at the Grand Hotel is one of Australia's greatest restaurants and in combination with the great value wines of the area, it means visiting Mildura is always one of the great pleasures of life. In 2003 he also set up his own paddle steamer, the *Avoca*, which sits serenely on the river and serves great lunches and snacks.

South Australia
Coonawarra

Here are the magic words for Coonawarra: terra rossa and cabernet sauvignon. The famous red earth of the Coonawarra, with its limestone sub-stratum, provides wonderful conditions for growing the equally famous grape. But wait, there's more: terrific spicy shiraz, reliably good sauvignon blanc and riesling and for the first fifty callers a set of steak knives. To the north is the much newer region of Wrattonbully which started as a sort of annexe but is starting to come into its own as a region for shiraz, cabernet sauvignon and merlot.

Best varieties cabernet sauvignon, shiraz and merlot.

Best recent vintages 1996, 1998, 1999, 2002.

Best producers Wynns, Katnook Estate, Balnaves, Rymill, Majella, Bowen Estate.

Best bet Hard to get to—easy to get around. Coonawarra is five hours' drive from Melbourne and four from Adelaide so a lot of visitors drop in for a day of rest on their way along the scenic route between the capitals. And once you're there, it's basically one long wine strip-mall, with most of the wineries strung out along a twenty-minute drive. What could be simpler?

Padthaway

As you'll see in the reviews section, Padthaway is one of my pet regions—a quiet achiever producing grapes for some of the tastiest wines in Australia. It is not, however, as well known as its famous neighbours Coonawarra and McLaren Vale, nor is it a major tourist destination and it's certainly not strong on cellar doors. Drive through it and appreciate it, but don't necessarily expect to find that there's a lot to stop for.

Best varieties chardonnay, shiraz, cabernet sauvignon.

Best recent vintages 1998, 2000, 2002.

Best producers Padthaway Estate, Browns of Padthaway, Lindemans Padthaway.

Best bet If you are the sort of tourist who can't drive past a grape vine without looking for the cellar door—or if you've lost your way and got thirsty between the Grampians and Coonawarra—you should drop into the very beautiful Padthaway Estate. It operates as a bit of a regional showcase for a few of the local producers, but the bulk of the fruit grown in Padthaway gets picked and then trucked away to equally scenic wineries in places like Jacob's Creek.

McLaren Vale

One of the great advantages of McLaren Vale is that it is less than an hour's drive from Adelaide so if things take an unexpectedly unbuttoned turn and the shiraz flows too easily, calling a cab back to town isn't out of the question. Expensive, of course, but not as dear as a tree through the windscreen. This region used to be seen as a bit dull and, well, middle of the road; today, McLaren Vale produces red wines, mainly shiraz or shiraz-based blends (the grenache blends are especially good), that are among the country's best.

Best varieties shiraz, cabernet sauvignon, grenache.

Best recent vintages 1996, 1998, 2001, 2002.

Best producers d'Arenberg, Tatachilla, Hardys, Ingoldby, Wirra Wirra.

Best bet McLaren Vale is not only handy to Adelaide, it's also within coo-ee of a beautiful coastline and stuffed with good restaurants. Quite a few McLaren Vale wineries also produce excellent olive oil—try Coriole for starters and keep your eye out for the locally grown almonds. Not only are the nuts incredibly more-ish (we don't often get a chance to eat really fresh nuts), the trees in bloom are simply breathtaking.

Adelaide Hills

Petaluma, Shaw and Smith, Nepenthe…Henschke have a cellar door in the Hills too. It's a pretty top-shelf line-up, producing some pretty top-shelf chardonnay, pinot noir and sauvignon blanc. The flip side is that a region capable of making such fine cool-climate chardonnay as this one is unlikely to be able to sustain a grape such as cabernet sauvignon, which ripens late in the growing season. Well, nobody's perfect…and you probably wouldn't be able to afford it anyway.

Best varieties sauvignon blanc, chardonnay, pinot noir.

Best recent vintages 1998, 2001, 2002, 2003.

Best producers Shaw and Smith, Petaluma, Nepenthe, Lenswood, Chain of Ponds.

Best bet Most of the vineyards are at least 500 metres above sea level, which is why they are cool as well as seeming cool (in the style sense). Go to Bridgewater Mill restaurant and warm up over an extremely fine meal. It's owned by Petaluma and has been voted South Australia's best restaurant several times in recent years. The Shaw and Smith winery is worth a go at the weekend—they don't just let you taste the odd glass, they give you an educational flight of wines to improve your mind. It's all very Adelaide, isn't it?

Barossa Valley

It is with due reverence and no levity at all that I call the Barossa Valley the spiritual home of the Australian wine industry. The big names tumble over each other: Penfolds, Henschke, Yalumba, Peter Lehmann and Wolf Blass for starters; even the original Jacob's Creek (the original Bin 65 is elsewhere, parked behind a Coles supermarket in the Hunter Valley). It almost doesn't matter what the Barossa is famous for—although for the record it's warm red wines made from cabernet sauvignon, shiraz, grenache or a blend—it's just famous, and has been for over 150 years. The cooler Eden Valley lies to the east, and produces wonderful riesling and fragrant, delicious reds that are sometimes a little more refined than the blockbusters from the valley floor. You must visit the Barossa at least once. It has its own 'Barossa Deutsch' culture, distinctive cuisine featuring German-styled smoked and cured meats and some of the best red wines anywhere.

Best varieties shiraz, shiraz, shiraz (and riesling in the Eden Valley).

Best recent vintages 1996, 1998, 2001, 2002.

Best producers Rockford, St Hallett, Saltram, Turkey Flat, Charles Melton, Richmond Grove.

Best bet Seriously, you should stay in the Barossa for a week to soak up the atmosphere, including a healthy dose of the local culture. If you visit the Apex Bakery in Tanunda and Schulz's butchers in Angaston, you can get the ingredients for greatest picnic in the world. Oh, and the wineries. One street alone, Krondorf Road, has three of my all-time favourites within a stone's throw of each other—Charles Melton, Rockford and St Hallett—and you'll have to do your pilgrimage to Yalumba, Peter Lehmann and Penfolds. Turkey Flat claims to have the oldest shiraz vines in Australia, Bethany has a wonderful view, Richmond Grove is a must-see…You take my point?

Clare Valley

Ah Riesling! Riesling riesling riesling… Clare is most famous for producing Australia's finest—always citrussy, floral and with a beguiling ability to age. But the Clare also produces wonderful shiraz and delicious semillon. It is the combination of cool afternoon summer breezes and the vineyards' altitude that makes this such a marvellous place to mature grapes. And the lovely rolling hills make it a beautiful spot to visit—about two hours' drive north of Adelaide and only an hour or so from the Barossa.

Best varieties riesling, semillon, shiraz.

Best recent vintages 1997, 1998, 2000, 2002, 2003.

Best producers Grosset, Pikes, Knappstein, Taylors, Tim Adams, Annie's Lane, Leasingham.

Best bet: Get on your bike! The Riesling Trail takes you through a multitude of vineyards and right past a couple of cellar doors; then at the end of the trail, when you feel you've had your exercise, someone will put you and your bike in a ute and take you back where you came from. If you get sick of cellar doors, go to the church door and visit the Jesuit winemakers at Sevenhill. It's the oldest existing winery in the Clare Valley and it still makes the sacramental wine it was set up in 1851 to provide (as well as some cracking table wines).

Western Australia
Great Southern

It's long—150 kilometres north to south—it's
wide—100 kilometres eat to west—and it's a
bloody long way from anywhere (four hours from
Perth). It had better be good, and it is. The Great
Southern takes in Mount Barker, Albany, Denmark
and the Frankland River and produces fine riesling,
chardonnay, merlot and shiraz. There are not many
people popping into the cellar doors but it's worth
the effort to go there since Great Southern also
takes in the magnificent Porongurups and some of
the most spectacular hardwood forests in the world.
After all there's (a little bit) more to a holiday than
just visiting wineries. This truly is a marvellous,
albeit damned isolated, place to go and see.

Best varieties shiraz, merlot, riesling and
chardonnay.

Best recent vintages 1998, 1999, 2001.

Best producers Plantagenet, Alkoomi, Ferngrove,
West Cape Howe, Houghton.

Best bet If you have come this far south you must
visit the township of Albany, Western Australia's
oldest settlement dating back to 1826. Whatever
you do, don't call it All-bany—it's Al as in
aluminium. It's also worth noting that some of the
very best wines in Western Australia are made using
fruit sourced from this region—so keep an eye on
the back label of your favourite WA wine and
check out its provenance.

Pemberton and Manjimup

For the serious tourer in the west: if you're coming
from Great Southern headed for Margaret River,
these two regions abut each other about halfway.
Still pioneer country—they've only been growing

grapes here for around ten years, so the place is yet to realise its potential. The best grape varieties haven't been fully sorted out as yet, but it looks like merlot, shiraz and verdelho could go pretty well.

Best varieties cabernet sauvignon, merlot, shiraz and verdelho.

Best recent vintages 1999, 2001, 2002.

Best producers Picardy, Salitage, Chestnut Grove, Gloucester Ridge.

Best bet Spectacular places these, with wonderful scenery and some great wines which might be a bit hard to find in bottle shops unless you live in Perth. What a shame you probably won't be able to get there. If you want to try some of the product anyway, your best bet would be to call the wineries direct and ask them if they have any distribution in your local area. One particular wine to look out for from here is the Chestnut Grove Merlot—definitely one of the five best merlots in the country at the moment.

Margaret River

I'm a bit of a rap for Margaret River. Hopelessly besotted, some say, but it's hard not to be. The area produces a couple of contenders for the title of Australia's greatest chardonnay (Leeuwin Estate and Pierro) and between Cullen, Moss Wood and a couple of others, they could probably raffle the cabernet sauvignon crown. You can put this down to an ideal climate, good soil, the right varieties and talented winemakers. If you then add beautiful scenery, great surf beaches and cellar doors to die for into the mix, it all makes pretty good visiting sense—just as long as you've got the do-re-mi. Cheap the wines of Margaret River, by and large, ain't. But in this instance, you get what you pay for.

Best varieties cabernet sauvignon, chardonnay, semillon, sauvignon blanc.

Best recent vintages 1995, 1998, 1999, 2001, 2003.

Best producers Leeuwin Estate, Moss Wood, Lenton Brae, Pierro, Cullen, Cape Mentelle, Voyager Estate, Vasse Felix, Devil's Lair.

Best bet Go to Margaret River in February if you're a music lover—that's when the Leeuwin Estate concert takes place, with performers like Ray Charles, Shirley Bassey and the London Philharmonic playing among the gum trees. Also worth a visit in Margaret River is the Caves House pub, great fun on a Sunday afternoon, the knick-knack shop at the Brookland Valley cellar door and the terrific restaurant at the Vasse Felix winery.

Queensland
Granite Belt and Mount Cotton

That's right—Queensland. It's not big, it's not well known, but the Queensland wine industry does exist and, despite the limited availability of appropriate climate and terrain, it's capable of turning out some pretty respectable product, mainly from the area known as the Granite Belt around Stanthorpe on the border with NSW. Almost every variety under the sun is grown up here, with mixed results. Shiraz can do quite well as can some of the white varieties like riesling and sauvignon blanc. Believe it or not there are now almost thirty cellar door outlets in the Granite Belt with the likelihood of more to come in the near future. And as the critical mass grows, of course the quality of wines improves. Although you couldn't yet stack most of the wines up against those from the more famous southern regions, rest assured it won't be long.

Best varieties shiraz, semillon, sauvignon blanc, riesling.

Best recent vintages 1998, 1999, 2001, 2002.

Best producers Ballandean Estate, Sirromet, Albert River Wines, Stone Ridge.

Best bet Check out the Sirromet winery at Mount Cotton—the most ambitious and by my reckoning most successful winery in the state. It has a 200-seat restaurant and is a terrific place to visit. Ballandean Estate near Ballandean township makes a very interesting sweet white using the German sylvaner grape, which is rarely grown in Australia, and it really is a wonderfully luscious, delightfully fresh sweet wine.

Tasmania

Last year we talked about a hat-trick of great vintages from 1998–2000, and 2001 turned that into a quartet. 2002 was a bit cool, but 2003 looks like it might be pretty good and the excitement is building. Tassie really is vastly improved and going places fast. There are some top specimens of chardonnay, pinot noir, pinot gris and riesling coming out of the Apple Isle, alongside the high-quality bubbles for which the place has long been admired.

Best varieties riesling, chardonnay, pinot noir, pinot grigio, gewürztraminer.

Best vintages 1998, 1999, 2000, 2001, 2003.

Best producers Tamar Ridge, Pipers Brook, Stefano Lubiana, Jansz, Clover Hill.

Best bet In the north, most of the vineyards cluster around the Tamar Valley and Pipers River, within an hour's drive of Launceston. Here you will taste some of the finest pinot noir in Australia and also some of the best bubbles. If you don't want to drive, you can park yourself at a little restaurant in Launceston called Stillwater. Let them bring you their wine list—outstanding Tasmanian wines at brilliant prices—and you'll never have to put the key in the car.

In the south there are several sub-regions in and around Hobart and it is here that you can find real diversity in style—from the relative warmth of Freycinet on the east coast to the southern-most region in Australia, the Huon Valley. You can—and definitely should—catch a cab from downtown Hobart to the Moorilla Estate complex. After lunch there wander up the road to Stefano Lubiano's place and beg for a taste of his top chardonnay and pinot noir. Or his bubbles, which are also great, or maybe his excellent riesling…

winespeak

Wine, like all industries, has its own jargon and it is probably as confusing to most people as computer-speak is to me. As soon as my IT guy says something about a byte I start thinking about lunch and pretend not to hear him. A lot of people in the wine industry think it's important to preserve this clandestine language to exclude the average person from unravelling the 'mysteries' of wine and winespeak. Well I hope the next few pages help take some of that pretentious mystery away.

By the way, about the pronunciation guides we've given alongside European names and expressions (except for those that are pronounced more or less as they are spelled)—the intention is to help you avoid embarrassment in the bottle shop. We can't guarantee that you will avoid embarrassment in the presence of a native speaker of French or Italian.

Acid

There are three main components in grapes that go into making wine. They are sugar, which gets fermented into alcohol, the skin and seeds, which add colour and tannin (to reds) and acid, which makes wine fresh and lively and sometimes tart and even sour. Acid is essential in all wines but is most noticeable in sparkling and young white wines—it is what makes these wines lively on the tongue and refreshing to drink. The two main acids in wine are tartaric and malic.

Alcohol content

Table wines in Australia range from around 6% alc/vol to 16%. The alcohol has the obvious function of making you feel either pretty good or pretty bad, or both in succession. But it also affects the texture of the wine in your mouth (see *mouth-feel*).

The amount of alcohol in the wine depends on two main things:

1. When the grapes are picked.

The riper the grapes are when picked the higher the level of potential alcohol in the end wine. More sugar = potentially more alcohol. Thus if you pick semillon in the Hunter Valley in January you might end up with a wine of only 10% alcohol. If you pick shiraz in the Barossa during May you can end up with a wine of 15–16% alcohol.

2. How sweet the wine is.

A winemaker can pick grapes very ripe but choose to leave a percentage of the sugar unfermented (this is referred to as residual sugar). The classic example of this is dessert wine that is picked ultra-ripe with a potential alcohol of 20% but is made only to an alcohol of 12%. It is the remaining sugar that makes the wine so luscious and sweet. A favourite wine of mine is moscato—these grapes are picked as normal for a wine around 12% alcohol, but the sugar is only fermented halfway, leaving a lovely sweet wine with only about 6% alcohol.

Aperitif

An aperitif is a drink served before a meal to stimulate the appetite and freshen the palate for the feast ahead. The classic aperitifs are sparkling wine or dry sherry. As a rule make your aperitif fresh, dry and not too alcoholic—rieslings and Hunter Valley semillons are perfect. My only problem with the aperitif is that I often enjoy it so much I keep drinking and forget to eat—what's it called then?

Balance

Balance is the key, the crucible—it is what all good wine should have. Balance means that there are no ugly bits sticking out. If the big shiraz smells only of barrels, it's out of balance; if the cheeky riesling is so tart it makes your mouth pucker, it's out of balance; or if the alcohol is so 'hot' it feels like you've just downed a shot of tequila, your balance is out of whack. Balance is when all the component parts of a wine come seamlessly together and none overwhelms the others. If only we could all have such balance in our lives!

Basket press

This is a term being used with greater frequency as winemakers and marketers try to instil a sense of heritage in their wines. After fermentation you need to press red grapes to extract the last of the juice and colour before further maturation in oak barrels. A basket press is an old-fashioned press that squeezes the grapes quite softly so you do not extract the bitter flavours from the skins and seeds.

Baumé (pronounced *bo-may*)

This is the French word that tells you how much sugar is in a grape, meaning how ripe it is and how far away from being ready to pick. Basically one degree of baumé converts into 1% alcohol if the wine is fermented to dryness. So if you go into the vineyard and find your grapes have around 13 degrees baumé you can be sure you will end up with a wine around 13% alc/vol if you let the yeast ferment all the sugar into alcohol.

Botrytis (pronounced *bo-try-tis*)

This is known in the wine world as 'noble rot'. It is a little fungus that eats into the grape and sucks out lots of the moisture, making the sugar and flavour concentration much higher. When the grapes are picked they look rather ugly and grey and the little juice you get when you press them is brown and treacly. Normally you will ferment around half the sugar and the result is a wine of regular alcohol with an incredible amount of unfermented sugar in it. Like all moulds, botrytis is at its best when there is a combination of heat and humidity, which is one of the reasons it does so well in warm regions like the Riverina. Botrytis loves attacking the semillon grape because it has a naturally thin skin, which enables the fungus to penetrate easily. Botrytis riesling is also increasingly popular and delicious.

Bottles

The normal sized bottle of wine is 750 mL but often you can find bottles that stand as tall as a small child. All of the really big bottles have biblical names.

1.5 L (two bottles)	magnum
3 L (4 bottles)	double magnum or jeroboam
4.5 L (6 bottles)	rehoboam
6 L (8 bottles)	imperial or methuselah
9 L (12 bottles)	salmanazar
12 L (16 bottles)	balthazar
15 L (20 bottles)	nebuchadnezzar

Bottle age

When a person says a wine has bottle age it simply refers—you guessed it—to how long the wine has been in the bottle. Most red wines will spend between six months and two years in oak barrels of some sort before being bottled, so if you are dinking a 2003 red wine right now, chances are it doesn't have a great deal of 'bottle age'. If you are drinking a 1973 red right now you should have called and invited me over.

Bouquet and aroma

A wine's bouquet and aroma mean what it smells like. That may not sound terribly sophisticated but you must remember that when we're talking about wine, if there is a choice between a simple word and a slightly pretentious one the pretentious word will always triumph. 'Proper' wine-tasters, unlike myself, will refer to the aroma as the fresh smells derived direct from the grape—these are the grapey, unadulterated smells you will find in the more aromatic varieties like sauvignon blanc and riesling. These tend to be unwooded styles. The bouquet refers to the smells derived from the winemaking art, so these will be smells associated with oak, yeast, wine age or the other flavours that can be controlled and created in the winery.

Brett *or* Brettanomyces

Brettanomyces is the 'fault du jour' for the wine aficionado. 'Brett', as it is widely known, is simply a form of spoilage yeast that can give wine a character that smells a bit like band-aids and makes it taste metallic. Some of Australia's most popular and expensive red wines have recently come in for serious criticism for having 'Brett' characters. Brett can get into a wine if hygiene and attention to detail are slack in the winery, if the winery doesn't use enough sulphur dioxide and if the high alcohol levels mean the good yeast can't ferment all the sugar so the 'bad' yeast starts to kick in. If you want to sound like a complete wine wanker at your next function, get a red wine in front of you and ask casually, 'Does anybody else notice the Brett character?' It doesn't matter whether you do or not because right now everyone has a different idea what it smells and tastes like and what wine it is in and what wine has none.

Cabernet sauvignon

Often referred to as the noblest of all grape varieties, cabernet sauvignon forms the backbone of many of the great red wines of Australia and the world. It offers aromas and flavours of blackcurrant and plum and often makes wines that can live for a very long time. The cabernet sauvignon grape has a pretty thick skin, so you can call it all sorts of names. This thick skin also means that when you make the wine you extract quite a lot of tannin (see *tannin*)—this can mean the wine will be quite dry and maybe a little bitter. If this occurs a percentage of merlot will often be added to the blend to soften the wine. Also these tannins can soften over time, which is why your higher-quality cab savs might need some bottle age before drinking.

Cabernet franc

Franc is cabernet sauvignon's oft-forgotten cousin but in many ways cabernet franc is the more noble of the two varieties. You see cabernet franc was around first (we're talking France here, many centuries ago) and cabernet sauvignon was only created when some cabernet franc and sauvignon blanc got up to some nookie in the vineyard. Cabernet franc is most commonly used as a blender in Australia, meaning that you might put 5–10% of it into a wine that will be based more on cabernet sauvignon or merlot. It tends to add a nice dark cherry character to a blend.

Cellaring

Not even 10% of wine sold in Australia is worth cellaring. It's almost all designed to be drunk within two years of its release date, so don't start making a cellar of all your favourite cheapies, they'll just go off and taste like vinegar. Only wine that sells for more than $15 or $20 a bottle will improve with age, and not all of them. The best bets among the whites are Hunter Valley semillon and Clare Valley riesling, while plenty of reds made from cabernet sauvignon and/or shiraz can cellar pretty well for a few years.

If you do have some old wine around by all means drink it, just don't expect to like it a great deal. Even wines that don't deteriorate with age will not necessarily change in a way that everyone enjoys. Old wine becomes more savoury and soft, and the juicy fruit, in-your-face character we like in young wines begins to fade. Other flavours might develop in their place, but if you like your reds nice and hearty and your whites fresh and crisp then keep drinking them young and turn your cellar into a jacuzzi.

Chardonnay

Chardonnay has taken over the world and in some countries they think chardonnay is in fact Australian for white wine. Chardonnay is a grape variety whose home is the Burgundy region in France—thus all 'true' white burgundies are made wholly from chardonnay. In Australia chardonnay is grown in just about every region but the best come from the cooler climate regions like Margaret River, Adelaide Hills, Mornington Peninsula and the Yarra Valley.

Cleanskins

Cleanskins—wines without any recognisable brand name, also known as house brands—are increasingly popular. These wines often offer excellent value for money, as they may well be the result of a winery wanting to clear out some excess stock quickly without having to brand the wine with their label. Some wines are produced by well-recognised winemakers who do not want you, the buyer, to know that they can make something so good, so cheap. On the other hand, I have also had some pretty ordinary cleanskins in my time which would be wines no winemaker would be proud to put their name to. If you are in the market to buy some cleanskins you must first trust your local retailer—let him or her know you can't be conned and that you'll happily buy the good ones but once burned by a dud you won't be back in the shop for quite some time.

Always buy a single bottle of a cleanskin before committing to a case. Chances are they will be a very attractive price if you buy by the dozen, but if you don't buy one bottle to try first, consider yourself warned.

Corks

Most cork comes from trees in Portugal and for the past decade or so there has been a war raging on whether natural cork or a simple screwcap is the best seal for wine. The cork industry is massive and is undertaking all sorts of offensives to convince drinkers that corks are best. The first thing they need to do is convince winemakers they can eradicate cork taint (see below). Most consumers see the cork as a natural part of the romance of wine and it will probably be a long time before a vast majority of wines are sealed with screwcaps. Personally, I'm a screwcap guy—I think they are far more sensible and risk-free, and to be perfectly honest, if a cork plays a significant part in your romantic life you should have a damn good look at yourself. The cork industry has started making serious noises about cleaning up its act as it sees more Australian and New Zealand wines moving toward screwcap. We will keep a close eye on cork quality over the next year.

Corked wine

'Corked' wine doesn't mean there are little floaty bits in the glass. Floaty bits won't hurt you, just fish them out with your fingers or a fork and get on with drinking. When a wine is corked, it is the cork itself that has been tainted by a nasty chemical known as TCA (trichloroanisole), believed to enter the cork somewhere in the cleaning process. The result is that the wine gets a mouldy kind of smell described variously as wet cardboard, mustiness, wet dog and so on. If you taste a corked wine at a restaurant or buy one from a shop, send it or take it back. Most producers will gladly refund corked wine and then get extremely cross with their cork supplier. Recent estimates say one bottle in a dozen might be corked, which is a pretty good argument for approaching some of the alternatives with an open mind (see *screwcap*).

Decanting

There are two reasons for decanting wine. One is to get rid of sediment at the bottom of the bottle; the other is to aerate it—let it breathe—before you serve it. For either purpose a water jug or any other similarly shaped instrument will do the job just as well as a crystal decanter. At home I use a jug I bought at the Reject Shop for $5 as my decanter.

As far as 'breathing' the wine is concerned, the simple act of extracting the cork half an hour before you start drinking is next to useless. The only part of the wine that is in fact 'breathing' is the tiny little bit at the top—maybe one per cent of the wine. If you want a wine to breathe you must aerate the entire wine, so you need to pour it all out into your water jug. The sort of wines you might need to do this with are young, rich, tannic red wines that might soften a bit if exposed to air. You never need to decant white wines.

Another word of caution—older wines can sometimes deteriorate quite rapidly after opening. With any wine more than ten years old, I recommend you decant it no more than twenty minutes prior to getting stuck in.

Digestif

This is the opposite to an aperitif. A digestif is a drink one has after dinner to encourage good digestion. The Italians like to drink very bitter-sweet digestifs like Averna. So do I, but Australia's most popular digestif is clearly a product called Victoria Bitter.

Disgorge

Sparkling wine (or champagne) is disgorged just prior to its final bottling. Disgorgement involves getting the dead yeast (see *lees*), the result of the secondary fermentation, out of the bottle quick smart before the bubbles disappear. This is done by riddling the bottles until they are upside down and all the yeast is in the neck of the bottle. You then snap-freeze the neck, pop off the top (which shoots a yeasty ice block out the neck), top up the wine with a little bit of something (see *dosage*) and then whack in the cork. That's disgorging.

Dosage

When you disgorge a sparkling wine (see *disgorge*) you lose a bit of the wine when you pop the little yeasty ice block out of the neck of the bottle. So you have to top the wine up with something. This is referred to as the 'dosage' and the exact composition of this dosage is often the best-kept secret in a sparkling wine house. Normally it is quite sweet so the resultant wine isn't too dry, sometimes it has a bit of brandy or spirit in it and with sparkling reds sometimes it can even feature old vintage port.

Fining and filtering

Fining and filtering are a couple of the more contentious winemaking practices—some winemakers think they are essential, others argue all they do is strip a wine of its inherent flavour. Fining and filtering will be done to a wine to ensure it is bright and clear not hazy or cloudy. Winemakers traditionally like to fine their wines with natural protein products like gelatin, skim milk, isinglass or egg whites—although if they use milk, fish or egg products they now have to declare that on the back label. This is in case there are some residual trace elements of these products in the final wine, which to be honest is highly unlikely if they are filtered properly. Isinglass is a protein extracted from the belly of the sturgeon fish in case you are interested.

Gewürztraminer

In Australia we have long referred to this white grape variety simply as traminer because the gewürz bit makes it too much of a mouthful. It is a variety native to the eastern parts of France and the slopes of Germany and both in Europe and Australia can make exotically flavoured white wines with great intensity. It can also make wines that smell like bath salts and taste like soap, so beware. Good gewürztraminer smells like fresh lychees and has a wonderfully slinky palate and plenty of acidity so it's not too soapy. Look for good gewürztraminer to come from the coolest regions in Australia like Tasmania and the Victorian Alps. It is also often blended with riesling to make the ever-popular, slightly sweet traminer riesling styles.

Grape varieties

In Australia we tend to name our wines after the grape variety, unlike in Europe where the wines tend to be named after a place. For instance in France, the home of chardonnay and pinot noir is the region of Burgundy, so if you buy a bottle of white or red burgundy you are expected to know that it is made from these grape varieties. One of the reasons Australian wine is so successful around the world is that we don't take this sort of knowledge for granted—we are quite prepared to tell people which grape variety or varieties have gone into the bottle. If a wine is called a cabernet merlot it is a blend of cabernet sauvignon and merlot—the first grape variety mentioned must always have the higher percentage in the blend.

Grenache

Grenache is a grape variety that I have often referred to as Brian Dennehy but perhaps I need to update that to Alan Dale. Why? Well to my mind grenache is a great supporting role actor but probably isn't up to the leading man role—it's just not good enough. So for mine, grenache is at its best in a blend with shiraz and/or mourvedre. Straight grenache, when it is left to star on its own, is a little like made-for-TV movies—quite pleasant but you'll forget what it was about as soon as it's finished.

Hermitage

Hermitage is a rather attractive town in south-east France that has become known as the 'home of shiraz' or syrah, as the French call it. For many years we used hermitage as a synonym for shiraz in this country, but that is no longer allowed due to an agreement with the European Union (see *labelling*). Even the most famous Australian hermitage—Grange Hermitage—is now simply labelled 'Grange'.

Labelling

Since the early 1990s there's been a major change in the way Australian wines are labelled. In the old days most of our wines were marketed with European names on the labels. Names like champagne, burgundy, moselle, chablis, hermitage, port and others. Not surprisingly, when our wines started being exported to Europe the people from these places got a more than a little upset about Aussie versions of their wines turning up on their own doorstep. To remedy this the European Union and the Australian Winemakers Federation got together and drew up an agreement that would see the Europeans free up their trade markets if we took the European place names off our labels. Thus today there are no more 'Aussie' versions of famous European wine styles. We can still name wines after grape varieties such as chardonnay, shiraz and cabernet sauvignon but not the aforementioned places. Nevertheless, we now have regions of our own that are gaining international renown like Coonawarra, Barossa, Margaret River et al.

If a producer states a place or a variety on a label at least 85% must have been made from/come from that place or grape. For instance if a wine is labelled 'Barossa Shiraz' at least 85% of the wine must have come from the Barossa and at least 85% must be shiraz. The other 15% could be cabernet sauvignon from the Coonawarra and it wouldn't have to be mentioned.

Lees

Lees is a nice word for dead yeast. It only takes a week or so for the yeast to eat all the sugar in the grapes, turning it into alcohol, and then with nothing more to do the yeast just dies. Nevertheless, yeast is still pretty useful in death. It falls to the bottom of whatever vessel the wine is in (oak barrel, bottle, tank) and in death still imparts, no surprises here, a yeasty character to the wine as well as some nice textural characters. The winemaker can choose to keep the wine 'on lees' for as long or short a period of time as he or she wishes. If the winemaker really likes a 'leesy' character the lees can be mixed into the wine every once in a while—this is known as 'lees-stirring' or 'battonage'. You will most often hear of lees in reference to sparkling wine where a wine may advertise the fact it has spent 'up to ten years on lees'. Sometimes if a sparkling wine has spent an extended period 'on lees' it might even smell a bit like Vegemite, which after all is merely a dead yeast extract.

Malbec

Malbec is a kind of second-division grape variety that will never really scale any great heights but has its uses as a blending component to add some mystery to a cabernet sauvignon-based wine. It has no really distinctive flavours or characters but can make quite palatable wine on occasion. Malbec makes grenache and cabernet franc look like superstars.

Malolactic fermentation

Often when we taste wine, most particularly chardonnay, the wine can have a creamy palate—all soft and buttery. The reason is an optional wine-making practice called malolactic fermentation, which is undertaken to transform the naturally occurring green apple-like malic acid into the softer, creamier lactic acid. This is done by adding the bacteria *Leuconostoc oenos*, but you didn't need to know that did you?

MLF is encouraged to occur in almost all red wines but is probably most notable in chardonnays where the buttery character can be most evident. Too much malolactic will make a chardonnay smell and taste like butterscotch.

Marsanne

A grape variety that really seems to have made a home in Victoria's Nagambie Lakes region. It can make some extraordinarily long-lived wines, most famously the Tahbilk marsanne. In its youth marsanne is quite a neutral variety and is probably best blended with its cousin roussanne and good friend viognier to make a complex, and often delicious white style.

Merlot

I have a bit of a problem with merlot. You see it's tremendously popular, but whenever I try a merlot, regardless of its price, I always find myself thinking how much better a shiraz, cabernet sauvignon or blend might be at the same level. I don't know why but I have this hard-core prejudice. I think merlot is a terrific variety to be blended with cabernet sauvignon and occasionally (very occasionally in fact) it can produce magnificent wine on its own but most of the time it just lets me down. In case you haven't read the rest of the book, my tip with merlot is to drink the cheap, fruity simple ones and save the big bucks for a good shiraz or cabernet sauvignon.

Méthode champenoise

There is no longer any such beast as Australian-made champagne: 'champagne' must come from the region of Champagne in France just to the east of Paris. Méthode champenoise is simply the method by which the folk of Champagne make their sparkling wine—by undertaking the secondary fermentation (where you add yeast and sugar to a 'base' wine—see *secondary fermentation*) in the bottle rather than in a big tank. Australian sparkling wine can be made from exactly the same grape varieties as champagne—pinot noir and

chardonnay mainly—and using the same method,
méthode champenoise. It just can't be called
champagne any more. See also *disgorging.*

Methoxypyrazine

This is one of those serious wine words spoken in
hushed tones by people 'in the know'.

Methoxypyrazines are basically flavour compounds
that give wine a herbaceous or capsicum-type smell
and taste. More often than not this is because the
grapes have not been allowed to ripen properly due
to the bunches being shaded by the leaves or the
growing conditions just being too cool. The most
common varieties to show a lot of this character are
cabernet sauvignon and sauvignon blanc. Some
people find these characters attractive; I say if you
want capsicum flavours you should be cooking not
drinking.

Mousse

Neither chocolate nor with horns, in wine the
mousse is what we call the frothy bit at the top of a
glass of sparkling wine (the 'head' if you like).
What you want is a nice consistent mousse that
sticks around as you keep drinking. If a glass of
bubbles has no mousse it could be because the
glasses aren't very clean or the wine you have
bought isn't crash hot—I always blame the glasses,
especially if I have paid. To make sure you get a
good mousse and bead (that's just the bubbles)
clean your sparkling wine glasses in the dishwasher,
not by hand and also make a small scratch at the
bottom of the inside of the glass so the bubbles
have somewhere to form.

Mourvedre

Mourvedre is a grape variety that originated in France's Rhône Valley and thus is featured in what we call Rhône-style blends or GSM's. The G is for grenache, S for shiraz and M for mourvedre. Mourvedre gives these wines a wonderful savoury, almost meaty, edge which on its own can be a bit too much. For many years in Australia mourvedre was known as 'mataro' which, let's face it, is a damn sight easier to say.

Mouth-feel

When wine people refer to mouth-feel they are talking about the texture of a wine, not just the flavours. Often the way a wine 'feels' in the mouth—is it soft and silky or tough and dry?—is as important as what it tastes like. Alcohol plays a major part in the mouth-feel of a wine—the higher the alcohol the heavier the wine feels on the palate.

Oak

Oak and wine go back a long way. For centuries winemakers have been maturing their wine in oak barrels for the same reasons people used to make ships out of oak: because it is a hardwood which is also supple, so it can be shaped without splitting, and, most importantly, it is watertight.

There are two main types of oak, French and American. Most people reckon French oak is better because it comes from lovely forests with exotic names like Limousin, Nevers and Limoges. French oak is also expensive—a single barrel that holds 225 litres of wine is likely to set a winemaker back a lazy $1200 or so. French oak tends to impart soft, savoury, smoky characters to both red and white wines, and it tends to make them a little more expensive too.

American oak is a little more 'in-your face' than its French counterparts and is most often used on big, brassy, ripe and fruity reds from our warm regions. American oak can cost around half the price of French oak, which is one of the reasons it has been so popular in Australia for many years.

All oak used to store wine is 'toasted' by exposing the inner staves to a naked flame. You can have barrels of light, medium or heavy toast and the choice of toast level will impact on how pronounced the toasty, oaky and smoky characters are in the finished wine. For a cheaper oak flavour, winemakers sometimes use things called oak chips, which are dangled in tanks like giant oak teabags to impart some oaky, toasty flavours.

Old vine

Often you will see a wine described as being sourced from 'old vines'. This is intended to impart an assurance of quality. As with 'low-yielding' there is in fact no rule that determines when a vine turns 'old', although most would agree that a vine has certainly become 'old' by the time it reaches its 40th birthday and there are those in the *Don't Buy Wine Without Me* office who could certainly empathise. Old vines produce lower yields of fruit with greater intensity of flavours, or so the story goes. Often the position, aspect, soil, irrigation, climate and vineyard management will be greater determinants of a wine's quality than the age of the vine, but certainly vine age can contribute to a wine's depth and complexity. The oldest living vines in Australia are most likely some of the old shiraz vineyards in the Barossa which were planted in the 1840s. For reasons not entirely known shiraz seems to be the grape variety that benefits most from vine age, or maybe we just have more old shiraz vines than other varieties!

Organic wines

Grapes grown in organic, biodynamic or at the very least environmentally sustainable vineyards are becoming increasingly popular in Australia and across the world, and this should be applauded. As for 'organic' winemaking; well this is an area of some conjecture. Adding a small amount of sulphur dioxide to a wine, for instance, is a common undertaking to make sure the wine doesn't oxidise or go 'off' but for some this means the wine is no longer 'organic'. Most wines have very little preservative added, in fact in Australia most winemakers will only add minuscule amounts of sulphur dioxide and ascorbic acid (vitamin C) to their wines.

Palate

Our palate is our mouth. Some people claim they have front palates, middle palates and back palates, I've even heard of a half palate, which is presumably somewhere in between! If a wine is very sweet as soon as you taste it, that is the front palate, if the wine is bitter as you swallow that is the back palate. That leaves the middle palate—one of the most elusive things in the world of wine. You will often hear a winemaker lamenting the absence of a middle palate, or the options for blending— such as merlot with cabernet sauvignon—to fill out the middle palate. The middle palate is the breadth of the tongue and the sides of the mouth. It is the key to a wine being 'mouth-filling', to being complex and to being 'long'. If the flavours of the wine hang around for a long time, that is a long palate.

Pigéage (pronounced *pee-jay-arge*)

When winemakers take off their gear and get right into the wine to stomp the juice and mush the skins, this is called pigéage. Not surprisingly, it is no longer widely practised in Australia—it's a little impractical with today's huge tanks, and most winemakers have no desire to drown, regardless of how good their pinot noir might be as the result of pigéage. This is great pity as diving into a vat of fermenting grapes is great fun, if terribly messy.

Pinot grigio / pinot gris (pronounced *pee-no gree-jo* or *pee-no gree*)

Here are two names for the same grape variety. Pinot grigio is the Italian name for the French variety pinot gris which is, in fact, a mutation of pinot noir. Pinot noir is a black variety while pinot gris is slightly grey and makes white wines. Pinot grigio produces wines of very distinct character, often flinty and savoury and smelling and tasting like pears. They are gaining popularity in cooler climates like the Mornington Peninsula and King Valley in Victoria and several parts of Tasmania.

Pinot meunier (pronounced *pee-no murn-yay*)

A cousin of the more noble pinot noir, pinot meunier is often added to a blend in sparkling wines in order to find the elusive 'middle palate'. It is rarely made into a table wine on its own although there have been a few produced by Best's in Great Western, Victoria. One of the funniest things I ever remember hearing at a wine function was someone questioning why the winemaker had added pinot manure to his wine.

Pinot noir (pronounced *pee-no nwahr*)

The most elusive and potentially the most exciting of all grape varieties. Pinot noir is like a siren, it calls for you, it seduces you and sometimes it just leaves you to crash on the rocks and drown. Great pinot noir is seductively smooth, deliciously long flavoured and incredibly complex. Average pinot noir is thin, weedy and light. It is a difficult grape variety to grow as it is extremely temperamental and will throw viticultural tantrums at the slightest change in the weather. As with so many things in our life, it is this difficulty, the sheer elusiveness of great pinot noir that makes it endlessly fascinating and at the end of the day, quite addictive. Pinot noir is also the key variety in great sparkling wines, where it is most often blended with chardonnay. New Zealand is currently the trendiest place for pinot noir in the world and in Australia the Tasmanians are going great guns as are several wineries on the Mornington Peninsula.

Preservatives

There are two preservatives generally added to wine in Australia. These are listed as Preservative 220 and Antioxidant 300.

Preservative 220 is sulphur dioxide, commonly referred to as SO_2. Sulphur dioxide is added to most fruit-based products like juice, dried fruit and wine to prevent the fruit from going 'off'.

The Australian industry closely monitors the levels of sulphur dioxide in wines and the maximum rate of sulphur dioxide permitted is harmless to the vast majority of the population. If you are an acute asthmatic or believe you are intolerant to sulphur dioxide consult your doctor.

Antioxidant 300 is ascorbic acid, which is more widely known as vitamin C. This is added to wine to ensure the fruit character is preserved and makes wine even healthier than you might have thought! Winemakers no longer have to declare if they use ascorbic acid on their back labels.

Riesling

Riesling is unquestionably one of the greats—possibly even the greatest of all the world's white grape varieties. It is capable of so many good things—fresh, crisp citrussy wine, sweet viscous wine, wine that ages, wine that is delicious young. Riesling has had a chequered history in Australia as for many years wines were labelled riesling when in fact they were more likely to be made from less noble grapes like sultana and gordo. This anomaly in labelling law has thankfully been addressed and today if you are drinking riesling, you can be assured you are drinking the juice of the riesling grape. The best rieslings in Australia come from the Clare and Eden valleys in South Australia but keep your eyes peeled for Tasmanian rieslings and rieslings from the southern parts of Western Australia—they can be absolutely brilliant.

Sangiovese (pronounced *san-jio-vay-zee*)

The native red grape variety of Tuscany and thus the vital ingredient in the famous wines of

Chianti. Sangiovese has been planted sporadically in Australia, often by Italian migrants longing for a taste of home. The grape makes savoury, slightly spicy wines that are at their best with a big bowl of hearty pasta. The grape is most often seen in Victoria's King Valley but can also be found in McLaren Vale, South Australia, and Mudgee, New South Wales.

Sauvignon blanc

This grape variety has the ability to polarise opinion like no other. You either love its herbaceous, grassy aromas and flavours or you think it's quite ghastly. For what it's worth I love it and reckon sauvignon blanc, on the whole, is the perfect summer drink. Look to the cool areas like the Adelaide Hills and the southern bits of Western Australia, and also look for good ones that are blended with a bit of semillon. Of course the most renowned region in the world these days for sauvignon blanc is Marlborough at the north of New Zealand's South Island.

Screwcap (Stelvin) closure

2003 has been the year the screwcap continued its incursion into the Australian wine market, with more white and red wines than ever being released without a cork. You will often see them referred to as a Stelvin closure, which is simply a particular brand name for a screwcap, and they are much the same as the caps that keep your vodka and scotch from spilling all over the place. Screwcaps are grouse, free of the potential problems of dodgy corks (see *corked wine*). If your friendly winemaker seals his or her wine with a screwcap it means they love you and don't want you to hate their wine simply because it suffers from a dud cork. You will see a lot of rieslings bottled under screwcap because their delicate aromas and flavours are the most prone to be affected by mouldy corks. This year we have also seen more sauvignon blanc, semillon and chardonnay released under screwcap and quite a few popular red wines. Don't be sniffy about screwcaps—they are great and should be encouraged.

Secondary fermentation

This is the process of getting bubbles into sparkling wine. The primary fermentation of wine transforms the natural grape sugars into alcohol by the addition of yeast—this is done in an environment where the carbon dioxide (a simple by-product) is allowed to escape. A secondary fermentation is the same thing but you don't let the carbon dioxide escape so it immerses itself in the wine—and *voilà*, you have bubbles.

Semillon

A vastly underrated grape variety capable of making dry and sweet white wines that can be among the very best in the world. My favourite white wine style in the whole of Australia is Hunter Valley semillon, which although rather plain in its youth, blossoms into something quite beautiful with around five years bottle age. Other great dry semillon styles are made in Western Australia where it is often the trend to add a little bit of the more herbaceous and racy sauvignon blanc to the blend. I am also the last person on this earth who still loves Barossa and Clare semillon too. Semillon also makes the greatest of all sweet wines when the grapes get affected by botrytis or 'noble rot' (see *botrytis*). In Australia, the best of these come from the Riverina around Griffith.

Shiraz

If I had to choose one grape variety to take with me to a desert island it would be shiraz. Among other reasons, it's such a dependable variety it might have a shot at growing on my island, where more temperamental varieties like pinot noir would likely give up the fight and die. Shiraz is as dependable as Steve Waugh once was and it makes great wines from most regions Australia-wide. But its sheer dependability shouldn't make you think it is merely a middle-of-the-road workhorse. On the contrary, shiraz is also capable of making the greatest of our wines, including Penfolds Grange and Henschke Hill of Grace. Look towards the Barossa, central Victoria, the Hunter, McLaren Vale and the sexy new regions in WA for our top shirazes.

Solero system

A solero system is what makes fortified wines like sherry, port, muscat and tokay so old and complex. It is a method of ageing wines by stacking barrels on top of each other and moving wine from the top (youngest) to the bottom (oldest). Each year the bottom barrels provide a lovely blend for bottling. The higher the solera, the older the wine is at the bottom.

Temperature

These are the temperatures generally
recommended for serving wine:
Sparkling wine and champagne 6–10° C.
White wine and rosé 8–14° C.
Red wine 14–20° C.
You can chill some red wines but the key is to
make sure that the wine is not too dry or bitter—
if a wine has any hint of bitterness the cold simply
makes it even more apparent. Pinot noir is often a
soft red wine, low in natural tannin, which means
it can be OK to chill. But I would only
recommend chilling pinot noir if you've paid less
than $15 for it—more expensive pinots lose their
subtle flavours when they are chilled. For the same
reason, many people will enjoy an expensive
chardonnay or old semillon more if they serve it
cool rather than ice-cold.

Terroir (pronounced *tair-wahr*)

This is the ultimate French wine term and it
cannot properly be translated into any handy
English phrase. The *terroir* is technically the
mesoclimate of the vineyard, or in layman's terms
the soil, lie of the land, wind, rain, sunshine,
humidity and local conditions that affect the
grapes and subsequently the wine's flavour. To put
it more simply, if you haven't the faintest idea why
a wine tastes like it does just shrug your shoulders,
give a Gallic harrumph and claim it is the mystery
of *terroir*.

Tannin

An often abused and rarely understood word that
really only applies to red wines—if you have

tannin in your riesling you have a real problem. Tannins are phenolic compounds extracted from the skins and seeds of grapes when they are mixed with the juice during fermentation. These tannins give red wine its drying sensation on the palate, and too much of it will make a wine taste bitter. If a wine is very tannic in its youth it should age well and get less bitter, because as a wine ages the tannins bind (polymerise) and fall out of solution, transforming themselves into the sediment we see in older wines. A small amount of tannin can also be extracted from oak barrels if a wine spends a long time ageing in barrel. Thus an unwooded white wine should have no tannin at all, while on the other hand, a full-bodied cabernet sauvignon that has spent two years maturing in oak will have plenty.

Verdelho (pronounced *ver-del-oh*)
Verdelho is a white grape variety native to Portugal. It grows well in warmer climates like the Hunter Valley, New South Wales, and the Swan Valley in Western Australia. It tends to make rich, fruity white wines that often have a touch of sweetness. Many people refer to verdelho as a chardonnay alternative as it can be nice and rich like chardonnay without the need for oak.

Viognier (pronounced *vee-on-yay*)
A grape variety to keep an eye out for and one rapidly gaining in popularity among Australia's more cutting-edge winemakers and the drinking cognoscenti. And for damn good reasons because viognier is quite capable of making really interesting wines with wonderful aromas and

flavours of apricot and honeysuckle. Viognier is also increasingly being blended with shiraz to give this classic red variety an extra hint of spice and a wonderfully aromatic perfume character. Normally no more than 5–10% would be added to shiraz. Varietal viogniers are being produced in the Eden Valley, Adelaide Hills and central Victoria.

Vintage

A wine's vintage is the year in which the grapes were harvested. In Australia a minimum 85% of the wine must be from the vintage that appears on the label. A non-vintage wine, most often sparkling wine, comes from any number of combined vintages and is therefore able to reduce the vagaries of the season and maintain a consistent style. In the wine industry, 'vintage' is the period when the harvest is coming into the winery and everyone works about twenty hours a day. Depending on the region, the vintage can start in January and continue through to the end of May.

Viticulture

Viticulture is the science and practice of growing grapes in the vineyard. It is not nearly as sexy as winemaking (oenology) but equally, if not more, important to wine quality. Remember, not even famous winemakers can make a silk purse from a sow's ear.

Yeast

You can make wine without grapes, without oak, without love or even without clothes, but you cannot make wine without yeast. Yeast turns grape sugars into alcohol and as a result should be awarded some sort of alcoholic Nobel Prize. The good type of yeast (which is a single-celled agent) which makes wine, beer and bread is a strain known as *Saccharomyces cerevisiae*, in case you were interested.

Yield

The back labels of bottled wine may often state that the wine has been made from 'low-yielding vines'. This means that each hectare of vines produces a relatively small number of grapes. In Australia producing fewer than ten tonnes of grapes from each hectare of vineyard would qualify as low yield, although there is no law that actually states what a low yield is. Popular wisdom holds that lower yields are better than higher yields because the grape flavours are more concentrated if yields are kept down. The easiest way to increase yields is to over-irrigate the vineyards in the summer–autumn growing period—this dilutes the concentration of flavours and makes for poorer quality wine.

Zinfandel

We don't grow a lot of zinfandel in Australia; however in the USA it is kind of like their version of our shiraz. For many years it was overlooked in favour of cabernet sauvignon but it is now making its triumphant return. In America zinfandel is also often turned into pretty rudimentary, pink 'jug' wine, widely referred to as white zin. We have pockets of zinfandel in Western Australia, the Adelaide Hills and McLaren Vale.